woodturning
projects

woodturning
projects

a workshop guide to shapes

mark baker

with a foreword by stuart mortimer

**GUILD OF MASTER CRAFTSMAN
PUBLICATIONS LTD**

First published 2003 by
Guild of Master Craftsman Publications Ltd
Castle Place, 166 High Street,
Lewes, East Sussex BN7 1XU

ISBN 1 86108 391 2

Publisher: Paul Richardson
Art Director: Ian Smith
Managing Editor: Gerrie Purcell
Commissioning Editor: April McCroskie
Editor: Stephen Haynes
Production Manager: Stuart Poole
Designer: Andy Harrison
Photographer: Anthony Bailey, except as listed on page 8
Illustrator: John Lovatt

Colour origination by CTT Repro
Printed and bound by Stamford Press, Singapore

contents

To my wife Sarah and daughters Eleanor and Hannah, who have put up with me not being around much while writing this book

acknowledgements

I would like to thank Kirk Boulton and Nick Davidson of Craft Supplies (UK), Ron and Gavin Joy of BWS, David Bates of Stiles & Bates, David Mounstephen of Yandles, Philip Wolsoncraft of P&D Timbers, and Bill Care, all of whom have helped immensely in tracking down the woods that I have needed for this book.

Special thanks to Paul Richardson, who gave me the friendly prod and encouragement needed to write the book.

Thanks to Bert Marsh, Ray Key, Chris Stott, Stuart Mortimer, Gary Rance, John Hunnex and Allan Beecham for allowing me to feature their work in the Gallery. They all have a generous, giving nature and a willingness to share that I hope to emulate. They have offered loads of encouragement during the writing of the book, for which a 'thank you' seems so little. Many others have also given encouragement and support, and it is greatly appreciated. An extra thank you to Stuart Mortimer for writing the Foreword and for being a constant source of wisdom and encouragement.

Thanks also to John Lovatt for creating the fine illustrations and for being there when I got stuck; to Stephen Haynes, the book's editor, whose diligence and patient manner were greatly appreciated, and who helped make the writing of this book as hassle-free as possible; and to Andy Harrison for his imaginative work in designing this book.

I thank the following manufacturers for their help with information about their products:

Australian Outback Timbers, BriMarc Associates, C. & M. O'Donnell, Chestnut Products, Craft Supplies Ltd (UK), Crown Tools, Hamlet Craft Tools, Henry Taylor (Tools) Ltd, Jill Piers Woodturning Supplies, Kel McNaughton, Record Power, Robert Sorby, VB Manufacturing, VM-UK and Woodchucker's Supplies.

To Harold 'Two Sheds' Cutts, a dear friend who sadly died before I completed this book.

photocopying

The designs in this book have been printed with generous margins so that readers may easily photocopy them to the required size for their own private use (see page 8); but please remember that all designs in this book are copyright and may not be reproduced for any other purpose without the permission of the designer and copyright owner.

foreword

Against the background of the woodturning boom which began in the late 1980s and continues today, a new crop of turners came to prominence. When I first met Mark Baker at one of the major woodworking shows, he was already teaching and demonstrating. He later became the product manager for a leading tool manufacturer, and it was clear that he was a developing talent with a lot of energy and several strings to his bow.

Mark is an excellent turner. He soaks up information, and has gained the respect of many leading turners. Meeting him at numerous shows and other events both at home and abroad, it was obvious to me that he had something special to contribute to turning. He also has a particularly valuable asset in his ability to communicate and analyse. As editor of GMC Publications' *Woodturning* magazine he is in a position to test virtually every new machine and tool on the market, and to monitor trends and developments within turning as a whole. With credentials like these, this book is especially welcome.

The book has been carefully planned to target as wide a range of turners as possible – not outright beginners, but those looking to advance their skills in the craft, and possibly questioning whether they are going in the right direction. Have you got the best equipment and tools for the job? How can you judge or improve your turning? Mark answers these questions by way of 50 projects – five of them covered in step-by-step detail – each accompanied by excellent illustrations and suggestions for alternative designs. Some of the tooling and techniques illustrated may appear advanced to some, but have a go: follow the instructions and you will advance your skills.

If you are a beginner, you can set yourself up in a very sound and safe working environment using the information given in the introductory chapters, then follow the projects at a simpler level. If you are a turner who likes a challenge, you may be inspired by these designs to go bigger, or thinner.

It may not be prudent to mention another author's book in a foreword, but I feel that I must. Keith Rowley's *Woodturning: A Foundation Course* is exactly what it says, and any turner who has used Keith's instructions will be able to continue in that vein and follow the projects contained in this book.

I congratulate Mark Baker and his supporting team on the production of this excellent book. Enjoy this book, and enjoy your turning.

Stuart Mortimer
August 2003

a note on the working drawings

All measurements are given first in fractional inches (to the nearest ½in), followed by millimetres. Because it would be impracticable to give truly exact equivalents, some dimensions have been varied to ensure adequate wall thickness, lid fit, etc. **It is therefore essential to stick to either metric or imperial units for each project; do not mix units.**

Heights are generally given from the same datum, relative to the initial or first-stage turning operation. Dimensions for subsequent turning operations are then given from a new datum, typically a top face or rim.

Where wall thickness is marked 'constant', this simply indicates that it should be as consistent as possible. (Note that on some designs the base thickness changes to accommodate inset foot details, etc.) If you vary the outside height of an item, you must remember to adjust the internal depth accordingly.

● **From base** means the measurement is taken from the lowest face of the item to be turned (which in some cases is the lid, rather than the whole piece).

● **Peak to peak** refers to the highest points of a feature which lacks distinct or defining detail.

● **Centre** means that one end of a dimension is taken from a centre position, such as halfway across a bead; **centre to centre** means that both ends of the dimension are taken in this way.

● **Angles** are given only as a guide, and are not critical, provided that matching angles are the same.

● **Scale** indicates the percentage to which the drawing has been reduced from the original article. To enlarge drawings to full size using a photocopier:

- ● from 75%: enlarge to 133%
- ● from 60%: enlarge to 167%
- ● from 50%: enlarge to 200%
- ● from 40%: enlarge to 250%.

photographic credits

Photographs in this book are by Anthony Bailey, © GMC Publications Ltd 2003, with the following exceptions: Mark Baker: pp. 11 (top right, middle right, bottom), 13–16, 19–23, 24 (bottom), 25–6, 28 (bottom), 29, 30; Mark Cass: p. 12; Axminster Power Tool Centre: p. 17 (top two); Robert Sorby Ltd: p. 17 (Sorby sharpening system); BriMarc Associates: p. 17 (Tormek); Terry Porter: pp. 70–3, 96–9 (step-by-step views); courtesy of Ray Key: pp. 172–3; courtesy of Stuart Mortimer: pp. 176–7; courtesy of Gary Rance: pp. 178–9; John Hunnex: pp. 182–3.

introduction

When I first starting turning I was fortunate enough to be able to attend many shows and visit a number of experienced turners. The people I met were patient and kind-hearted, and explained many of the 'mysteries' and so-called secrets to me. Some even popped in once in a while to see how I was getting on. Most of them specialized in no one aspect, but could lend their hand to anything, and if they were offered a job that required a skill they did not have, they learned it rather than turn away the job and lose the money.

Without exception, all said that turning should be enjoyed, but that the only way to get better was to practise, and when you think you have had enough, practise some more. I took this on board and read all I could on the subject, copying and making pieces. I was allowed to borrow templates, and practised making them.

Had I not had access to this advice, it would have taken me a lot longer to become proficient. It was their kind words and encouragement that taught me to experiment, and have fun doing so.

There are many great books available that help turners to get started, or focus on a particular aspect, but few that cater for the turner who has learned the basics of cutting and holding work, but is looking for ideas and shapes to work with. I have aimed this book at such turners. I make the assumption that you have acquired the basic skills, and have a chuck which works in both compression and expansion, a set of lathe jaws, and a selection of tools and finishing products.

There are, all told, 100 designs in this book. All of them have drawings, and 50 of them have fully annotated diagrams for you to work with. I have covered some projects in step-by-step detail, but for each

design there are hints and tips on how to create the turning, a list of tools needed, and comments on the woods used. I have not tried to cover everything: I have not ventured into the application of colour, carving, inserting fillers, combining different-coloured woods, and so on. These are areas you can explore for yourself later. This book is intended to be a practical workshop guide to shapes of varying difficulty and how to make them; it is not a treatise on design.

There will be designs here that you like and some that you do not. This is good. No one likes all designs, and deciding what you don't like, and why, is a starting point for creating your own designs. So by all means copy the designs shown, but if there is a feature you do not like, adapt it using the knowledge you will gain as you work through the projects.

Each drawing is scaled so as to fit on the page. The easiest way to scale them up or down as required is to use a photocopier which enlarges and reduces.

Many professional turners have developed their own styles and designs. I have tried not to copy, but may have inadvertently come close to someone else's work, in which case I apologize. When you are looking at shapes and turnings all day, it is inevitable that you assimilate the information seen. The trick is to adapt and modify it so as to make it your own. No one can lay claim to 'owning' a cove or ogee, but when it comes to a particular placement of certain details and so on, this is a different matter – it would be wrong to copy work exactly and pass it off as your own. All of the turnings shown here are adapted from a variety of sources, as are everyone else's. The most important thing is to practise turning, and have fun.

safety

I don't want to sound nannyish and overbearing, but it is all too easy to be blasé and forget that some aspects of turning can be dangerous. Here are some gentle reminders:

● Always match the speed of the lathe to the work. The bigger and more out of balance the work, the lower the lathe speed should be; the graphs below are a guide. Make sure that a low speed is selected *before* starting the lathe.

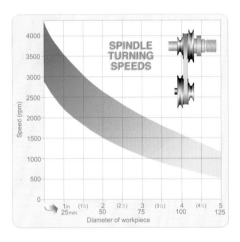

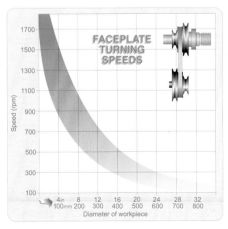

● Keep tools sharp: blunt tools are dangerous because they require more pressure and may behave unpredictably.

● Don't wear loose clothing when turning, and make sure that loose hair is tied back out of the way

● Protect your eyes and lungs at all times. This is necessary not only when turning, but also when sharpening tools on a grinder or cutting wood with a bandsaw or chainsaw.

● All wood dust and grinding dust is potentially hazardous to health. Try to get as good a finish as you can straight from the tool, which will lessen the need for aggressive sanding; but you also need to have some method of dealing with the dust as close to the source as possible, by using either a portable extractor or a fan which removes the dust outside the workshop. You also need to protect your eyes: goggles are OK, but a respirator with integral face shield is better, although granted it is more expensive. Ambient air filters are good to collect the very fine dust that can stay airborne for days.

● Work in a tidy environment. A friend of mine once tripped on a trailing lead and tumbled into a piece of machinery. Keep leads off the floor, and tidy up regularly.

● Make sure that there is good lighting, both ambient and directional. Being able to see the work clearly will pay dividends not only from the safety point of view, but also in the quality of work.

● It is always advisable to take a shower after spending time in the workshop. Some woods can cause allergies and skin

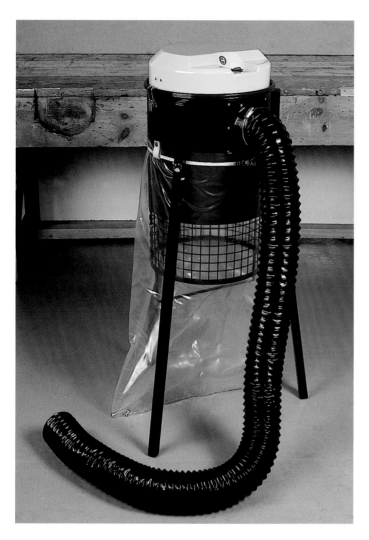

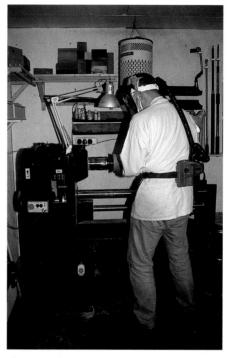

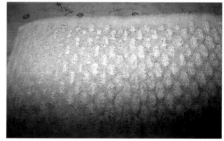

sensitization, which may take a long time to become apparent, so it is important to remove dust as soon as practicable.

● Dispose of oily cloth or paper towels at the end of the day by soaking them in water and placing them in a metal container. This will prevent fires caused by spontaneous combustion.

● Make yourself aware of the products you have in the workshop. Many familiar finishing products contain solvents that may have long-term effects with prolonged exposure.

● Ensure you can turn the lathe off quickly in the event of an accident – a remote switch is great, as is a foot switch for the lathe. A workshop isolator switch will prevent children from going in and starting machinery.

● Ensure that your work is secured on the lathe at all times. Wet wood can compress very easily and work loose in a chuck. Heavy cutting can move work a little after a while.

● Don't turn when tired, or when using medicines which cause drowsiness. The risk of making a silly mistake is too great.

● Have fun while turning, but think safe.

ABOVE LEFT A portable extractor that can sit near the lathe and be connected to machinery such as bandsaws

TOP Using a respirator, with an ambient-air filter on the ceiling just behind the lathe. Note also the good directional lighting

ABOVE The dust collected in the ambient-air filter from just one bowl

LEFT It's surprising how many finishes we have in our workshops

ideas

RIGHT Some of my sketches, playing with a shape to see what can be created. You don't need to be able to draw well

ABOVE The forms used in ceramics and glass can also be used in turning. This ginger jar could become a hollow form or, if you use the lid as well, a lidded box or jar. You will see this shape used on pages 56–7

RIGHT Keep an eye out for details on other turnings that may be useful to you, such as this oak baluster

One of the questions I encounter most often when demonstrating is: 'Where do your ideas come from?' Don't worry: we all have trouble to start with.

When I started turning, I read all I could about the subject. I copied shapes from books and from other work I had seen. This allowed me to practise shapes that I knew to be successful. After a while, I became aware that certain shapes, such as ogees and spheres, can be elongated, squashed or stretched. This enabled me to manipulate the repertoire of shapes I had copied, and create variants of them. This is a natural progression from the copying stage, and is very exciting.

This 'playing' will expose you to different varieties of turning, and you may find you prefer one type to another. Many turners specialize in certain styles or types of turning. For instance, David Ellsworth was one of the first to perfect the techniques needed for working through small openings on hollow forms; his work is exquisitely created and executed. Bert Marsh creates the most delicate of shapes, that defy all perceptions as they balance on a small base. Ray Key's explorations of shape in his platters and bowls are masterful and well worth studying. Stuart Mortimer's work epitomizes the spirit of experimentation. All of these have been major influences on my work. You may even become well known yourself for particular styles of turning in the future.

Not everything I created was a success, but I started to understand why things did or did not work, as the case may be. I still do not always get it right. In any case, not everyone will agree on what shapes look good – our perceptions are different.

I once heard someone say (I think it was in a film) 'You look without seeing.' I think the best advice I can give is to be observant of the shapes around you. It may be a flower, fruit or vegetable, a piece of glass, ceramic, stone or metal, or it may be other turnings. There is a myriad of forms that turners can usefully draw upon for ideas.

I keep a sketchbook in which I put down my thoughts at the end of the day – well, most days. Like most people, I forget to do this from time to time, but it takes minutes and is a good habit to get into. I do not feel it right to copy someone else's work directly. Though this is fine to start with while learning, you should never pass off other people's ideas as your own; always acknowledge the originator. You can, however, copy a shape from nature with impunity.

When I jot down shapes at the end of the day, I have had them in my mind for a while and cannot remember all the detail of the original, but I have the gist of it. This ensures that I have not copied exactly. Once I have an idea on the sketchpad, I doodle and see what I can do with the shape. Now I am not a gifted draughtsman or artist, but these doodles are enough for me to get going and work out what the profile will be, barring any foul-ups during turning, or flaws in the wood which may mean altering the design somewhat. Sometimes I get as far as 'plan G'.

As your skills progress, the permutations of what can be created from a piece of wood are worked out largely in the mind. Because you have practised and manipulated shapes over some time, there is a visual and mental catalogue of shapes that can be drawn upon. This is not possible unless you look at shapes and play with them. A sketchbook is a good point to start, as is reading as much as you can on the subject of shape.

This egg-shaped water feature works well as a form. The rounded bottom causes it to 'lift' off the surface, so it does not look immovable. The basic shape is used for the hollow form on pages 126–7

The shape of this simple cup-like blue-glazed pot is ideal for use as a turned bowl. See if you can spot which of my bowls is based on this form

A stone or pebble might not seem the most promising of shapes, but this one has a squashed appearance that suggests a good shape for a hollow form. Have a look at the hollow form on pages 120–5 and see what you think

This ripening fig is similar in shape to a tear or a raindrop, and could easily be adapted for turning

tools and equipment

I have already said that I have aimed this book at those who have a basic understanding of how to turn, and I have assumed that you have a basic set of tools and equipment. But here's a run-down of the equipment used in the projects.

lathe

There are so many lathes of various sizes and prices available now, that one is spoilt for choice. I have a small workshop, about 17ft long by 10ft wide (about 5 × 3m), and, with the other equipment I needed to fit in, could find room for only one lathe. Space was not the only factor; money also played a big part. I did not want to make do with a lathe that would not be adequate for what I wanted to do in the future, or flexible enough to tackle the wide variety of jobs that I currently work on – and it would have to last for a very long time. (Many readers with young families will identify with this.) So I bought a big lathe with tailstock assembly. It's large, solid, and will last. It's not perfect, but then we all have our own requirements, and your criteria may be quite different from mine. However, a good lathe should be well built and solid, so as to dampen vibration. It will have:

● a good speed range – a minimum of four speeds from 250 to 2000rpm (variable speed is great, but not essential)
● a minimum capacity of 12in (305mm) diameter
● a good, strong, threaded spindle on which to mount the chucks
● through-bored head- and tailstocks with a Morse taper in both to take drives and centres, and so on
● a minimum ¾hp motor
● a toolrest assembly which is easily moved and adjusted.

It is entirely up to you whether you choose a lathe with an integral stand, or fit it to a workbench; but whatever the lathe is mounted on, it must be sturdy enough to minimize vibration.

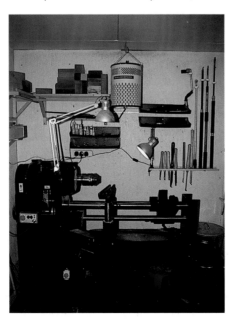

My VB36 lathe enjoys good lighting, and everything is to hand

chucks

Again, there are many types available, but the most commonly used are scroll or geared chucks. These usually consist of a key-operated mechanism that can move the jaws to grip onto a spigot, or into a recess in the work. One set of jaws will not do everything, so choose a chuck whose jaws can be removed to allow others to be fitted; 2in (50mm) jaws are a good place to start, and are often supplied as standard with a chuck. It's also advisable to buy a chuck that has a removable insert or backplate, so that, should you ever change lathes, you can buy a new insert or backplate to suit the spindle thread, rather than having to sell the chuck and get a new one.

There are various sizes of chucks to suit various sizes of lathes. If you have a small lathe, it is best to buy a compact chuck. If you buy one that is too heavy, you can ruin the bearings of the lathe.

accessories

I also use a screw chuck to mount the work initially. This can be fitted directly onto the spindle of the lathe, or some models are now available that fit into the jaws of the chuck.

A revolving centre and a two- or four-prong drive spur are essential for between-centres work. The drive spur locates into the end of the work and drives it round, whilst the revolving centre is used to support the work at the other end as it revolves.

bandsaw

Though not essential, this is a handy piece of equipment to have in the workshop. I use it to dimension wood from planks or logs to whatever size is required.

I recommend that any bandsaw you purchase should be of the two-wheeled variety; these give a longer blade life, and have a minimum depth of cut of 8in (200mm). Anything less, and you will be severely restricted in what you can cut.

LEFT Chucks fitted with 1½, 2½ and 4in (38, 63 and 102mm) jaws. Some have dovetail sections; others have serrated teeth, which give a better hold on wet wood

BELOW Jumbo plates or jaws fitted to the chuck enable platters and bowls to be held while the bottom foot, recess or spigot is cleaned off

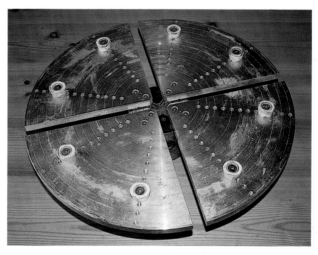

A compact chuck. Even though it's a little lighter than the others, the grip strength is just as good

Clockwise from left: a two-prong drive spur, a screw chuck and a revolving centre

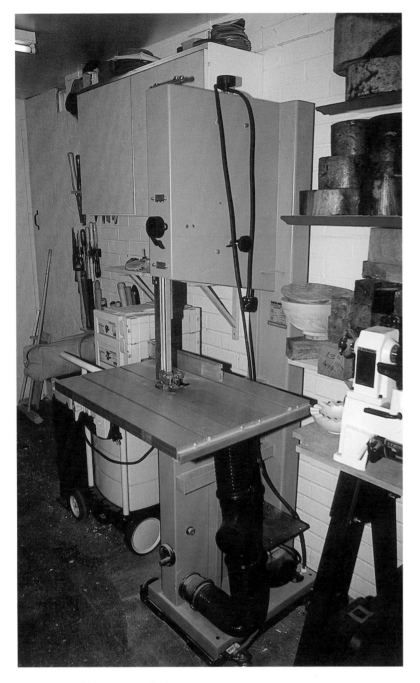

callipers and gauges

Gauging wall thickness with your hand is fine, so long as you can reach the part you need to get to, but sometimes you can't. Callipers come in all shapes and sizes, and are available from most good turning suppliers. It is worth having a selection.

adhesives

It's also a good idea to have some PVA adhesive, epoxy resin and cyanoacrylate of various viscosities in the workshop. These three adhesives will cover most eventualities that a turner will encounter.

ABOVE Adhesives of varying kinds and viscosities

sharpening

Probably the most commonly used item to sharpen turning tools is a bench grinder. Aluminium oxide grinding wheels are preferable, to avoid excessive heat build-up; because they do not clog as easily, they run cooler than the grey ones which are often supplied with the less expensive grinders. In addition to this, most bench grinders have been designed

ABOVE A bandsaw with a large capacity is very handy and makes light work of dimensioning

RIGHT AND FAR RIGHT Callipers of various sizes and shapes for measuring wall thicknesses, internal hollows, spigots. etc.

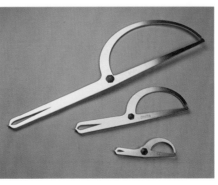

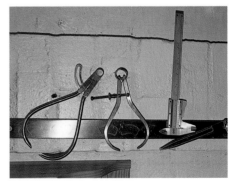

for engineers, to remove metal rapidly. Turners need to sharpen, not remove masses of metal, so, if you can afford it, purchase a slow-speed grinder running at about 1400rpm as compared to the 3000rpm of some grinders. This will improve control no end.

Most grinders do not come with a sharpening jig. There are dozens of makes of jig available, but a rising and tilting platform type will cater for most of the grinds you need.

An alternative to the bench grinder is a wet grinder, in which the stone revolves in a trough of water at much slower speeds. This type of grinder can also be fitted with a honing wheel to create a super-sharp edge. A unit of this type is equally useful in a general-purpose workshop for cabinetmaking and carving tools.

In addition to a bench grinder or wet grinder, I recommend having a diamond hone. These can be used to restore an edge on turning tools and other cutting tools very quickly, and are invaluable when sharpening tipped tools that require only a light honing.

A slow-speed grinder with wheels 1½in (40mm) wide

The O'Donnell sharpening jig

The Tormek water-cooled sharpening system with honing wheel

The rise-and-tilt platform and the fingernail profiler from the Robert Sorby sharpening system

turning tools
spindle turning

This covers a wide range of work, from
lace bobbins made from 5 × ¼ × ¼in (125
× 6 × 6mm) blanks, to hefty 8ft × 8in × 8in
(2.4m × 200mm × 200mm) blanks to
make four-poster beds. With very few
exceptions, blanks for spindle work have
their grain running along the length and,
apart from size, the tools and techniques
to turn them are more or less the same.
Spindle-turning tools comprise two main
types, gouges and chisels, with the
introduction of a third kind – scrapers –
for cleaning internal cavities, as in boxes.

faceplate turning

This term covers work performed at the
headstock end of the lathe, without
necessarily using the tailstock.

Although the term is still in common
use, faceplates themselves are not used
much now, given the wider choice of
mounting options based on the use of
chucks. Because making bowls is so
popular, this type of work is quite often
referred to as 'bowl turning'.

In faceplate work the grain of the
wood usually runs across the face of the
blank. This gives the workpiece greater
strength, and generally shows off the grain
of the wood to better effect, while
promoting more efficient use of timber,
and allowing larger blanks to be produced.

In view of the almost universal use of
chucks and devices other than faceplates,
a better term would be 'headstock
turning'. However, the point for now is to
make clear the distinction with spindle
turning. The cutting tools fall into two
types: bowl gouges and scrapers.

hollow-form turning

The grain on this type of turning can run
either along its length like a spindle, or
crossways as in faceplate turning. This type
of turning requires us to work through
restricted openings in pieces such as vases.
Vases may also have undercut shoulders
which cannot be accessed with straight
tools. The tools used for this work are as
described for faceplate or spindle turning
depending on the grain orientation, but
with the addition of specially designed
tools to work through the restricted
openings, and some cranked designs for
the undercuts.

notes on individual tools

Some of the tools listed here are available
from various manufacturers, and I have
not mentioned specific makes. However,
some specialized types are made by only
one manufacturer, and I do identify these.

spindle roughing gouge

These are made in various widths from
about ½in (13mm) to over 1½in (38mm),
and you should choose the size which
approximately matches the intended
work. The shape is the same, irrespective
of size. They are often forged from flat bar,
but can be milled from round bar.

As the name implies, they are used to
'rough down' a piece of spindle work
initially; that is, quickly remove the surplus
wood to approximate the required shape.
A suitable sharpening angle is anywhere
between 30 and 45°, and the tool is
ground square across the end.

spindle gouge

This type of gouge is intended for further refining the shape of the workpiece, and for forming round-bottomed recess cuts, or *coves*, as they are known. It can also be used to create a multitude of other curved shapes such as ogees or beads, and decorative features such as finials.

Spindle gouges come in a wide variety of widths, from ⅛in (3mm) to about ¾in (19mm), and the size used must be matched approximately to the size of the detail required. Again, all sizes share a common shape, which differs from the square-ended roughing gouge by having a swept-back or fingernail profile on the cutting edge. This gives you more freedom to manipulate the tool in the cut.

Like roughing gouges, spindle gouges can be made from round bar, or forged from flat bar. The most widely available is the round-bar type. Like the spindle roughing gouge, this tool is used with the bevel rubbing on the wood. A suitable sharpening angle is anywhere between 30 and 45°.

bowl gouge

At first sight this is similar to the spindle gouge, but closer inspection will reveal a deeper, narrower flute, with a more substantial thickness of metal for the shaft. This is because a bowl gouge has to be able to operate deep inside the workpiece, where it is not possible to give the cutting tip close support from the toolrest; it therefore needs to be made stronger to withstand the extra strain, and to resist vibration.

Sizes range from about ¼in (6mm) to ¾in (19mm). In the UK, the width is measured from the inside wall of the flute to the far outer edge of the bar, so a ⅜in (10mm) gouge is actually about ½in (13mm) diameter in total. In the USA, the whole diameter of the bar is measured.

This tool is also used with the bevel rubbing, and a typical sharpening angle is about 45–60°.

LEFT From top: ⅜in (10mm) fingernail-profile spindle gouge with 30° bevel angle; ½in (13mm) fingernail-profile spindle gouge with 40° bevel angle; ¾in (19mm) spindle roughing gouge

BELOW Top: ⅜in (10mm) square-ground bowl gouge with 60° bevel angle
Bottom: ⅜in (10mm) fingernail-profile bowl gouge with 45° bevel angle

From the top: ⅛in (3mm) parting tool; ⅜in (10mm) beading and parting tool; ¾in (19mm) skew chisel; ½in (13mm) round-edge skew chisel

skew chisel

Again, this comes in a range of sizes from about ¼in (6mm) to 2in (50mm). It is so called because the sharp end is ground to a lopsided or skew angle. Skew chisels have two functions: the first is to produce a smooth surface finish by using a planing action, and the other is to make incised cuts which can be used to form convex beads, V-cuts or decorative lines, or to clean up end grain. The planing action gives an excellent clean cut on end grain.

Skew chisels can be made from flat, oval or round bars. Irrespective of what style is used, the cutting action is the same. A suitable sharpening angle is about 30°; the skew angle is about 60°. This, like the gouges, is a bevel-rubbing tool.

beading and parting tool

Usually quite small, these are generally made from square stock between ¼in (6mm) and ½in (13mm), and are used to 'part off' the work from the waste section. They are also used to shape beads, incise lines, create tenons or spigots, and make V-cuts on the surface of the workpiece. The sharpening angle for this tool is between 30 and 45°. Belonging to the chisel family of turning tools, it is used with the bevel rubbing.

There are narrow versions of this tool, usually rectangular in section and typically ⅛–¼in (3–6mm) thick, that are just referred to as 'parting tools'.

The fluted parting tool can also be used to make small beads.

From the top: ¼in (6mm) round-nose scraper from round bar; ¾in (19mm) French-curve scraper; ¾in (19mm) side-cut scraper; 1½in (38mm) dome-end scraper; 1½in (38mm) curved-end scraper; multi-tipped hollowing tool by Robert Sorby; tipped shear scraper by Robert Sorby. The multi-tipped hollowing tool is shown here in scraping/shear-cutting mode; when fitted with a different cutter (supplied with it), it becomes a hollowing tool

scrapers

As the name implies, the cutting action is a scraping one most often without the bevel rubbing, and scrapers come in a variety of shapes. They are still seen by some woodturners as 'not proper cutting tools', but, while they should not be used as a substitute for gouges, they are effective shaping tools and easy to use. They do have a place: for material removal and shaping in certain contexts they may be the right tools for the job. They usually range in size from ¼in (6mm) to 2in (50mm). The cutting end can be almost any shape, and the bevel angle can be anything from 45 to 80°.

For the insides of bowls, goblets and boxes, a French-curve scraper is good; for the outsides of bowls, a square-across scraper is ideal.

specialist hollowing tools

Working through restricted openings means that it is not always possible to use a gouge, with the bevel rubbing, to profile the inside. Specialist tools have been developed that are designed to cut cleanly inside these hollows, and some are shaped to undercut shoulders, as on a bottle or vase form. They can be broken down into two types: scraping tools and shielded cutting tools.

Both types come in straight and cranked (swan-neck) versions, and in various lengths and blade thicknesses. The scrapers may be either solid or tipped. Shielded cutting tools have a hood over the cutting edge that can be adjusted to limit the depth of cut. Theoretically these tools cut more quickly and cleanly than the scraping type, especially in wet woods, but they are more expensive.

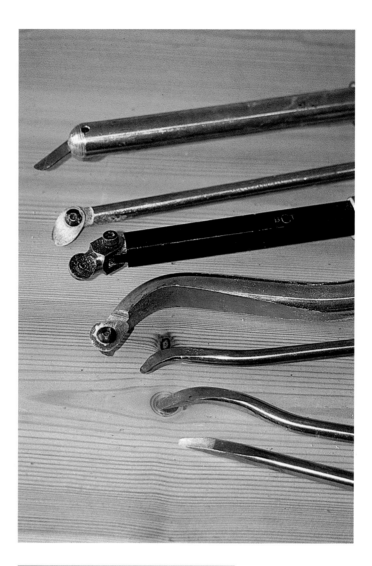

ABOVE Scraping hollowing tools. From the top: Multi-tipped hollowing tool by Robert Sorby; Probe tipped hollowing tool by Robert Sorby; BCT hollowing tool and shear cutter; Hooker cranked cutting arm from the RS2000 series by Robert Sorby; three different sweeps of hollowing tool by Kel McNaughton

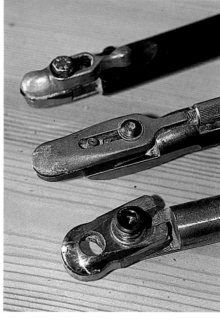

RIGHT From the top: Proforme Hollow Master by Woodcut; Exocet hollowing tool by Link Technology; Big Brother hollowing tool by Hamlet Craft Tools (this also accepts scraper tips)

finishing

Finishing is vital to a piece of work: the form can be turned to perfection, only to be ruined by slapdash finishing. All work needs to be finished in some way, even if it's a tooled finish. The finishing process usually involves sanding or abrading the work to remove blemishes, followed by the application of a sealing coat of some sort. Here are a few pointers.

RIGHT Sanding the foot of a bowl held in jumbo jaws

BELOW Power-sanding a natural-edged burr piece

abrasives

Nearly all work is sanded or abraded. Sandpaper gave us the word 'sanding', but has long been superseded by superior products called 'abrasives' that cut more cleanly with less heat build-up, last longer, and are generally flexible. These are the qualities of a good abrasive for the turner.

It is best to get as good a finish as possible straight from the tool before sanding begins. Some woods finish so well from the tool that you may be able to start at 240 grit. Others are not so kind, and will require starting with a coarse grade. Whatever grade of abrasive you start with, a good tip is to sand at a low lathe speed, keeping the abrasive moving across the work at all times. If you sand at high speeds, the abrasive does not cut; instead, it burnishes the surface, and heat builds up which can result in heat checks forming. It is important to progress through the grades and not skip any.

Turners generally use two types of sanding technique. One is hand-sanding, where the abrasive is held in the hand against the rotating or stationary work and traversed across the surface to remove blemishes. The other is power-sanding. For this you need to have an arbor with a hook-and-loop face onto which the abrasive is fixed, and a method of driving it, usually a drill. The revolving arbor is then traversed across the surface of the revolving work. Best results are achieved by having the arbor run in contra-rotation to the work on the lathe.

This method of sanding is devilishly quick, and a light touch is required so as not to create unwanted furrows.

An effective technique, which I first saw used some years back by Ray Key, is to sand using paste wax as a lubricant. Ray applies the wax to the finish-turned piece prior to sanding with fine abrasive. The dust and wax then combine to form a slurry which gets pushed into the grain and acts as a grain filler. No further finishing is required, other than burnishing with a clean cloth.

I saw Ray use this method on a box, but the technique can be applied to all types of turning, using either paste wax, oil or water as a lubricant. I use oil most of the time now.

The one drawback of this method is that it can only be used on wood of uniform colour. On laburnum, for example, which has cream sapwood and dark heartwood, the sanding slurry will be dark and will contaminate the light areas.

Simply turn the work to the required profile and dry-sand any major blemishes away. Apply a coat of oil or wax to the surface, and sand at a low speed. If you see dust forming, you need to apply more lubricant and work through the grades of abrasive. Once sanded, use a clean cloth to apply a further coat of the oil or wax, then burnish to a smooth finish. This technique is used in many of the projects in this book.

power buffing

This can be used to clean up a surface or apply a finish to it. A polishing mop is loaded with either wax or micro-abrasive 'soap' from a block, and is then mounted on a pigtail mandrel which can be held in a chuck on the lathe or in a drill. You can either move the work against the rotating wheel, or traverse the mop, held in a drill, across the surface of the work.

I first saw this system being used in America, but it has caught on quickly around the world. I certainly use it a lot.

ABOVE Power-sanding arbors from Gill Piers and Tim Skilton, pre-cut power-sanding discs from 3M and Performance Abrasives, and a roll of Astra Dot hook-and-loop-backed abrasive from which to cut your own disks

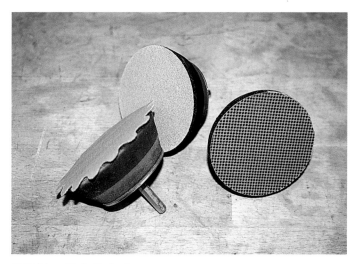

ABOVE Arbors fitted with abrasive

LEFT Various grades of abrasive in sheet and roll form for hand-sanding, by Hermes, Vitex, Astra Dot and Platin. A Simon Hope sanding rod is also shown; this has a hook-and-loop-faced ball to which abrasive is attached. It is available in handled and swan-neck forms to work in places that cannot safely be reached by hand

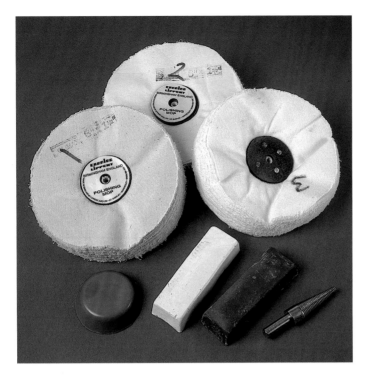

Two buffing mops with mandrel, blocks of abrasive and wax. Polishing mops are available in many sizes and shapes. This kit is from Chris Stott

Polishing mops loaded with a clear paste wax and an abrasive compound

The work is sanded to the required standard, and then I apply oil or melamine. After the required number of coats has been applied and allowed to dry, I power-buff the surface, usually with the mop loaded with a fine abrasive compound and held in a cordless drill. Some compounds, such as Diamond White, are sold in blocks. Others, like Chestnut Products' Hard Burnishing Cream, or EEE-Ultrashine from U-Beaut, are creams or waxes. The mop is moved over the revolving work, making

sure it does not stay in one spot too long, until all the surface has been covered and any streaks or minor blemishes removed.

After power-buffing, I either burnish the surface with a clean cloth, apply another coat of oil or wax by hand, and burnish again; or take a second polishing mop, this time loaded with paste wax or with carnauba wax from a block, and traverse this across the work to create a high-gloss finish. This really is a fast and efficient way of achieving a fine finish and removing tiny blemishes from the surface.

finishes
oils

Oils are amongst the most versatile of wood finishes. They penetrate, nourish and can help to seal the wood. The lustre built up after a few coats (cutting back between coats with ultra-fine abrasive) is second to none. There are oils that will finish to a high gloss, such as Organoil Hard Burnishing Oil, while others, like lemon oil, create a satin-matt finish that does not alter the colour of the original wood. Some are food-safe, such as those made from citrus oils or tung oil; many are water-resistant. My favourites are:

● 'Danish' oils, which are based on tung oil and can be used on all types of woodwork. I use them for products that receive a lot of handling. If the oil is a little thick, I thin it with white spirit (mineral spirit) to a runny consistency so that it penetrates and seals the wood. Danish oils can be used indoors and out. The only downside is that they darken the wood.
● Organoil Hard Burnishing Oil and Ecowood Oil, which are based on natural products including citrus and eucalyptus oils. These leave a lovely silky lustre without darkening the wood too much.
● Sunflower oil. This inexpensive oil is ideal for finishing items that will come into contact with food. It's a little bit thick, but works well if you apply it with a brush, wait for a few minutes, then burnish it with a clean cloth.

If you intend to sell items or give them away as presents, beware of finishing them with nut oils. Nut allergy is on the increase, and if you do not use nut oils you will not have to remember to warn people about them.

surface finishes

sanding sealer

Sanding sealers are used to seal and prepare the surface of the wood prior to the application of a wax or oil finish coat. Cellulose-, shellac- and acrylic-based products are available. The shellac-based type is more commonly used in the furniture-making industry than in turning, and can take quite a long time to dry. In any case, this product has to a large extent been superseded by the cellulose-based sealer, which dries much more quickly and provides a more durable base than the shellac-based product. The acrylic sealer is a more recent innovation; it dries quickly and is designed to be less toxic than the other varieties.

cellulose lacquer

Available in both spray and liquid form, cellulose lacquer dries quickly, and many layers can be built up to form a hard, durable surface that is resistant to moisture and handling. The rapid drying can be a problem if you apply it by hand, rather than by spraying. It is easy to leave brushmarks or streaks from the cloth, which will mar the surface unless they are burnished out. I tend to thin a new tin of lacquer by 30–50%, as I prefer to apply a series of light coats to achieve a streak-free surface.

acrylic lacquers

Available both in spraycans and in liquid form, acrylic lacquers are water-based products that are less toxic than the solvent-based alternatives. The sprays are particularly useful for intricate shapes that are difficult to finish by hand. Many light applications are better than one thick one.

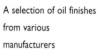

A selection of oil finishes from various manufacturers

friction polish

Friction polish is a shellac-based product that also contains carnauba wax. It is applied with a cloth to stationary work, then the lathe is switched on and the cloth is moved across the work to friction-dry the polish, which in turn melts the wax across the surface. The trick is to keep an even pressure and move the cloth at an even rate across the work to avoid creating streaks. This is one of the reasons that friction polish is used mainly on small work, such as boxes, where a constant pressure can be maintained. Larger work tends to be finished with other products. Friction polish forms a high-gloss finish, but is not durable and will fade quickly if handled. Melamine coated with wax will give a more durable finish.

A selection of surface finishes

A lozenge of pure
carnauba wax

A selection of waxes

Waxes come in various
colours and shades; the
type most commonly
used by woodturners
is clear

polyurethane finishes

These are often referred to as varnishes, but this is not accurate. The transparent or amber shades known as 'clear' and 'natural' are the most commonly used, but you can now buy coloured variants. Because they are slow-drying, they are best used on furniture rather than turnings.

waxes

Waxes and oils have been used as finishes for centuries. The most common form of wax used was beeswax. It still is used, but is often blended with other materials to make it more durable. The mix of ingredients varies from one manufacturer to another. There are some which dry quickly; these are used more often than not by the furniture industry. Those that are referred to as 'paste waxes' are usually spirit-based, and dry a little more slowly. These paste waxes can also be used as sanding lubricants; the method was described on page 23.

Some waxes are being produced now that do not have the spirit solvents; instead, they use citrus or eucalyptus oils as solvents.

Turners also use blocks of wax, which can be either pure beeswax or carnauba, or a mixture of the two. These are used by applying the block to the work as it spins in the lathe, traversing it across the surface, and then buffing with a clean cloth. This evens out the wax and creates a film finish.

burnishing products

I have mentioned that some finishing products are prone to streaking, and that power buffing with micro-abrasives is a good way of getting rid of these blemishes. However, you don't have to power-buff with these products: you can apply burnishing creams and waxes by hand, using a cloth. It takes a little longer, but is just as effective.

Burnishing creams and waxes

finishing the bottoms of turnings

While on the subject of finishing, I would like to share a couple of techniques for finishing the bottoms of your turned work.

After turning the inside and outside, it is sometimes desirable to finish the very bottom of the turning to clean it up and remove chucking marks, or hollow the spigot to create a delicate foot which would have been too fragile if made at an earlier stage. One method is to use jumbo jaws on the lathe chuck, as shown below. If you do not have jumbo jaws, try the method shown on the opposite page.

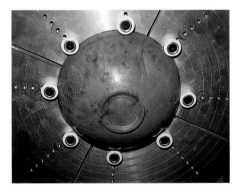

Jumbo jaws or plates can be used to hold the bowl either on the outside or inside of the rim, depending on the shape. This method gives full access to the bottom, so you can turn, sand and apply a finish unrestricted

Turning the bottom without jumbo jaws

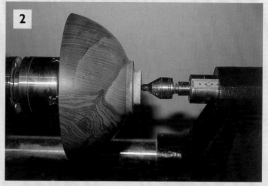

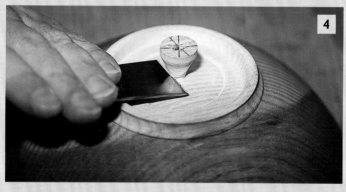

1 Fix a piece of ply or scrap wood on a faceplate or screw chuck, mount it on the lathe and turn a shallow dome on the face

2 Lay a thin piece of fabric over the face of the dome, place the inside of the bowl over this, then bring up the tailstock and locate the revolving centre in the centre of the spigot or recess on the bowl. Apply just enough pressure to prevent the work slipping when turned

3 Set the lathe to a low speed – about 300–500rpm, depending on the size of the work – and create the detail or effect you need. Sand as far as you can reach

4 A little spigot will be left where the revolving centre was located; this is removed with a carving tool once the work has been removed from between centres

5 The rest of the base is sanded and finished as necessary

woods

ABOVE A selection of
woods from around
the world

BELOW Dimensioned
sections ready for turning
into boxes, goblets
and vases

Wood has a place in everyone's heart. You only have to look around the house to see that we have an affinity with it: we use it for furniture, floors, walls and many other things besides.

Turners have the opportunity to work with woods that most other woodworkers do not. We often prefer the oddments that are discarded by cabinetmakers: the bits that have unusual grain, the small burrs (also known as burls), the boughs and crotches of trees that large timber

companies do not consider commercially viable (although some firms know that turners will pay a fortune for that rare or exceptional piece), but in a turner's mind can be more precious than gold. We often seek out the odd bits where there is a hint of something different, and relish the challenge of getting the best from it. I must admit to having as much fun hunting out timber as I do turning it. I will travel miles to get hold of some with exceptional figure and patterning, and then spend a long time working out how to get the best from it. But it's a sad fact that no wood is cheap. Even 'found' wood needs to be worked on before it is usable, and you can expect to pay a premium price for figured wood of any kind.

Even if we are not using highly figured wood, each piece is subtly different. The turned shape may well be identical, but each item you make will be unique.

You can buy wood in various forms: boards, pre-dimensioned blanks both round and square, or even complete trees. The cheapest way of buying wood is as trees or logs, which you can dimension yourself; the only problems are transport and storage. The next cheapest is as

through-cut boards. Again, you can cut what you want from these, though you will be restricted of course by the diameter and thickness you purchased. The most expensive option is pre-dimensioned blanks from a specialist supplier. Obviously, not all of these options are available for all woods and all localities. How you buy will depend on your budget, requirements and storage facilities. To start with, until you are versed in timber conversion, I would recommend buying blanks from a reputable store. The staff will be helpful, and you can see clearly what you are buying. I do not have the space to store large logs, but have a wide selection of through-cut boards and pre-cut blanks.

However you source your wood, some of the timbers mentioned in this book are difficult to obtain. It is always worthwhile to get to know your specialist wood supplier, and try to introduce yourself to the local tree surgeons too. Both will be more willing to help if they know you are

a turner, and might even be happy to let you know if they have come across something special.

I have made a deliberate choice in this book to use only woods sourced from Europe, Australia and North America. This is not because I object to the use of timbers from tropical rainforests and other sources – indeed, I use many such species myself – although there are real issues that need to be addressed concerning sustainability and the proper management of the areas from which they are extracted. However, I would encourage turners to explore the beauty of the timbers that are native to their own locality, and learn how to turn these to their fullest potential before exploring premium-priced materials from further afield. There are many exciting, 'exotic' species and variants on our own doorstep. I have had the pleasure (if that's the right word for some of the nasty, dusty and obnoxious woods I have

Ready-cut blanks for turning into bowls and hollow forms

This rough-turned bowl has distorted during drying and is now ready for final turning. I have left enough wall thickness to allow for this distortion

encountered) of turning over 150 species, with many variants such as crotch, burr and ripple forms, yet there are many from my own country that I have yet to try.

The issue of drying is a subject that could fill a book in its own right. Suffice to say that many of the projects in this book require timber that is stable and will not shrink, warp or twist once turned. The list of Further Reading on page 188 includes some useful books that cover this subject and more.

I have used a combination of drying or seasoning methods to stabilize the woods used in this book. The most common technique is to rough-turn the blank first, removing the bulk of the waste wood but leaving enough to allow for final turning at a later stage. The piece is then left to dry and stabilize for three months to a year,

depending on the size. The piece will invariably be out of shape after this time, but, provided I have left enough wall thickness, I will be able to turn the work to its finished shape and thickness. To gauge the wall thickness for the initial turning, my rule of thumb is that for a piece 6in wide by 3in thick (150 x 75mm) there needs to be a wall thickness of ¾in (18–20mm). This can be increased proportionally as the wood size increases.

But, no matter what wood we work with and how it's been seasoned, some woods are easier to turn and work with than others.

The alphabetical list that follows is intended as a practical guide to the turning qualities of the woods used in this book, and the features you may encounter when you buy a piece.

apple *Malus sylvestris* **Europe**

All fruitwoods are dense and close-grained, so they are ideally suited to turning. All cut easily, whether wet or dry. Apple, in my experience, is not prone to massive variations in colour, except in the roots or burrs; otherwise, it has a nice cream to orange coloration with a distinctive grain patterning. It cuts cleanly with both gouge and scraper, and if you are fortunate to come across a burr – which will be highly coloured and is very likely to have swirling grain patterns – then that also cuts well. Fruitwoods are ideal to turn with, and if you can get hold of them they are well worth experimenting with.

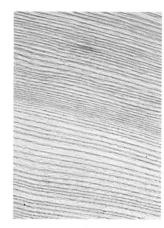

Apple

ash *Fraxinus excelsior* **Europe**

Ash is a wonderful timber to work with. It has a pronounced and rather open grain, but cuts well with sharp tools. It has a creamy colour and is available in large sizes, so platters are a possible use for this wood.

Some ash has a brown or greenish colour to it, known as 'olive' ash. Although it is the same species, this is usually denser than normal ash, and is also nice to turn. The figuring and coloration in olive ash can be quite stunning. Though it is not unheard-of to find massive pieces that are all olive, it is more likely that you will find streaks of olive running through an otherwise plain piece. The contrast between the two can be very striking.

Olive ash

Ripple ash, as you can see from the picture, has ripples running across the grain; when a piece is held in the light and moved, the ripples shimmer. Ripple figure is highly prized in both ash and other woods, so expect to pay a hefty premium for rippled wood of any kind. These ripples can be a little tricky to finish, as the grain tends to pluck out a little; take very light cuts with very sharp tools, and you should be OK.

Ripple ash

beech *Fagus sylvatica* **Europe**

Beech is a great wood to work with. It is close-grained, excellent for kitchen utensils and so on, but is usually rather bland to my way of thinking. It is cream to buff-brown in colour with visible grain flecks, cuts well with all tools and is not too expensive to buy, which makes it a good wood to practise on. It is available in large sizes, and is easily obtained from good timber suppliers.

Beech is one of the woods that are prone to spalting. This is where fungi colonize the wood, staining it attractively as they go. The trouble is that the wood will also be colonized by other fungi that rot it, so spalted wood can be somewhat soft or 'punky' (too soft to cut cleanly) if it has been left too long before converting it to usable sizes. There are some reports that spores from the spalting may have a causal link to respiratory ailments, so take

Ash

Spalted beech

precautions to eliminate both dust and spores from the workshop. If the spalted wood is soft, it may require stabilizing with sanding sealer to harden it prior to final turning, in order to get a clean cut.

Spalted wood can be quite dramatic, with black and blue lines running through the piece, and this is when I think beech comes into a class of its own for turning.

Beech will sometimes, but not often, form burrs. These tend to be highly coloured – pink, in this case – with swirling grain, and may contain small knots. The piece shown here cut easily with all tools.

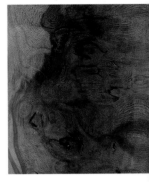

Beech burr

birch, masur *Betula alba* **Europe**
This wood, being quite soft, is easy to turn. It is a cream colour, with dark squiggly flecks and tiny tight swirls running through it. Usually bought as part of a trunk or bough, it is rarely available in diameters above 14in (350mm), and is highly sought-after. Because of the small sizes available, hollow forms, natural-edge pieces and boxes tend to be the items most commonly turned from it. If you can get hold of a piece you will have great fun working with it.

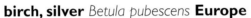

Masur birch

birch, silver *Betula pubescens* **Europe**
Silver birch is a timber that is often overlooked as far as turners are concerned. It has a reputation for being a little soft, prone to picking out and generally quite boring. I find this a little sad. The wood is cream to buff in colour, admittedly a little soft in patches, but cuts well with sharp tools.

It is available in reasonably large sections and can display some nice figuring, such as the ripple shown here. Where there is rippling, the wood does pick out a little, but the small amount that occurs can be cleaned up with abrasive.

Ripple silver birch

The spalted silver birch shown here is the most highly spalted piece of wood that I have come across. There was quite a bit of degrade, so I stabilized the wood by immersing the part-turned piece in melamine sanding sealer, thinned by 50% with an appropriate thinner. It was allowed to soak for some time and then removed and allowed to dry before finish-turning. I think the effort was worth it.

box elder *Acer negundo* **USA and Europe**
A large-growing tree, which gives creamy-white or buff-coloured wood. It is quite common to find red streaks and markings as shown here, although I have seen pieces with much more pronounced colouring than this. It cuts well, but this piece was also somewhat spalted and this made it a little soft.

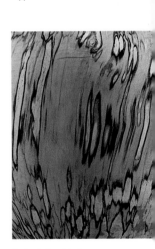

Spalted silver birch

Box elder

boxwood *Buxus sempervirens* **Europe**

Usually a creamy-yellow colour, it is dense, a dream to cut with all tools, and holds very fine detail. It is one of the few woods on which you can cut a screw thread cleanly without breaking. Only available in small sections, it is difficult to dry in the log without splitting. Since it is usually sold as a branch, this can be a problem.

The piece used in this book was spalted and had beautiful green-blue streaks running through it.

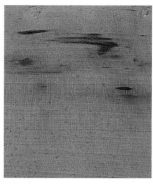
Boxwood

Spalted box

cedar *Cedrus libani* **Middle East**

Varying in colour from dark yellow to orange-red, cedar is available in quite large sizes, so you may be able to get a piece from which you can turn a platter. It is quite light, cuts well with sharp tools, and has a strong but pleasant smell. This piece was cut from near a bough, and had the branch knot and some reaction wood in it. (Reaction wood is the area adjacent to the bough, where the wood is either compressed or stretched.) The knot area was two or three times denser than the reaction wood, but cut and finished well. The reaction wood, which has some great figure in it, was a little tricky to cut cleanly with a scraper, but shear-scraping at 45° sorted it out.

Cedar (figured)

cherry, European *Prunus avium* **Europe**

A beautifully grained wood that is easy to turn with sharp tools. Burr forms tend to be of a swirling grain type, rather than pippy burrs. As with apple and other fruitwoods, the roots can also be turned if they are of sufficient size.

Sweet chestnut (figured)

chestnut, sweet *Castanea sativa* **Europe**

Sweet chestnut has an open grain, similar to ash, and is a yellow-brown colour with a subtle grain pattern. It is easy to work with sharp tools, and rarely presents any problems. It is available in large sections, which makes it ideally suited for platter work. There are often darker streaks running through the piece. I do not know whether this is caused by fungal growth, as with the beefsteak fungus in oak, but these areas seem to be denser and closer-grained than the non-coloured wood – similar to olive ash.

Cherry

cypress *Cupressus* spp. **Europe**

The sapwood of this interesting timber is a cream colour, and the heartwood a reddish-orange with a pronounced grain pattern. This is a softish wood to work with, and somewhat oily. It cuts well with sharp tools, and when cut has a strong smell that is quite pleasant. I think oil finishes work best for this wood. I have known melamine finish to flake off after a while, although I have not had this problem since I started thinning it down by 50% with the recommended thinner.

Cypress

Damson

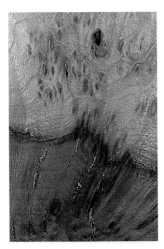

False acacia burr

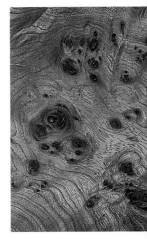

Elm burr

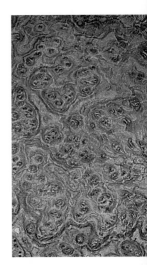

Goldfield burr

damson *Prunus cocomilia* **Europe**

Because it usually has a lot of colour in it, to my mind this is the king of the fruitwoods available in the UK and Europe. It cuts well but is not available in very big sizes. Not a commercial timber, though if you know any friendly tree surgeons they should be able to keep an eye out for you.

elm burr *Ulmus procera* **Europe**

Elm has an open grain, a cream to brown sapwood, and heartwood that is brown to greenish-brown with a pronounced grain pattern. It cuts well with sharp tools. The burr form of elm is highly prized, ranging from swirling grain and tight pippy burr through to the larger cat's-paw patterning.

false acacia burr
Robinia pseudoacacia **Europe and USA**

Yellow-green to light green-brown when freshly cut, this wood will mellow quite quickly to a deep green-brown colour. It has quite a coarse grain, but cuts well with sharp tools. The burr form is not uncommon, and is quite spectacular. It usually has tight clusters of small pippy knots with swirling grain around them.

Goldfield burr *Eucalyptus* spp. **Australia**

Goldfield is a region in Australia, and there are many trees from the eucalypt family that grow there. There are literally hundreds of different types of eucalypt around the world; some are fast-growing, while others, including those of the Goldfield region, are very slow-growing, which probably accounts for their hardness. This piece is typically dense and hard, and was bought as a carbuncle-type growth, ideal for use on natural-edge work. These burrs are sold by weight in Europe, and can be quite expensive, but as an occasional treat, they will reward your efforts with some of the most amazing grain patterns and figuring you are likely to come across. The colour variations in the eucalypts can be quite dramatic, and range from the deepest reds through to the brightest yellows. The sapwood is often discernibly different in colour, and makes a nice contrast with the darker heartwood.

This piece did not cut well with a gouge: it produced only chips. It cut better with a sharp scraper, which took off ribbons of fine shavings. So be prepared for the unexpected, and experiment with the tools to see which ones cut best. Beware of heat-checking caused by over-aggressive sanding.

horse chestnut burr
Aesculus hippocastanum **Europe and USA**

There is a marked difference between the sapwood, which is cream, and the heartwood, which is brown. The wood has quite an open grain structure, but cuts well with sharp tools. However, it will pick out a little if they are not sharp. The spalted variety

Horse chestnut burr

goes soft very quickly, so be careful what you buy. If the wood is very dry, it will produce a lot of dust when cutting. I think it is best turned when the moisture content is about 15%. In this condition it does not produce much dust, but will move a little as it dries fully.

jarrah burr *Eucaylptus marginata* **Australia**

This is another eucalypt, and one that is very well known. Jarrah is hard and dense, and is used for all manner of work; because of its density it is one of the favoured woods for railway sleepers (railroad ties). The sapwood is a cream colour and the heartwood ranges from soft pink through to deep maroon-brown. The burr form usually consists of tightly formed clusters of knots which are easy to turn when wet, but can raise a lot of dust if cut when dry. It can be very hard to cut, and will chip out during cutting, so requires a gentle touch with sharp tools.

Jarrah burr

laburnum *Laburnum* spp. **Europe**

One of the deepest-coloured woods we have in Europe. The sapwood is cream, while the heartwood is a deep brown with subtle subtints of green and red. The contrast between the two is great. Sounds like a description of a wine, doesn't it? Close-grained with a marked grain pattern, it cuts well, holds detail, but is not available in very large sections.

lime *Tilia vulgaris* **Europe**

A favourite for carvers, lime or linden is not so well known amongst turners. The wood is close-grained, and cuts well and easily. It also holds fine detail, even though it is not dense. It can seem a rather bland cream colour, showing little grain patterning, but this is why carvers like it. For this very reason, it is an ideal wood for when you wish to explore shapes and form without being distracted by pretty grain and figure.

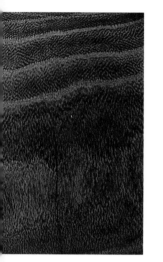

Laburnum

Lime

madrone burr *Arbutus menziesii* **USA**

A moderately close-grained wood with a reddish-brown heartwood; the sapwood is just a little lighter. It cuts nicely, even though it has an erratic grain, and the burr is in the form of striations running along and across the grain.

maple, American
Acer saccharinum and related species **USA**

American maple is a lovely wood to work with. It is close-grained, cuts well with all tools – this applies to all the maple varieties listed here – and usually has a pinkish tinge to the pale brown colouring. It is a little softer than the field maple from Europe, and is available in large sizes.

Madrone burr

American maple burr

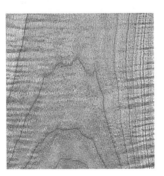

Ripple maple

European maple

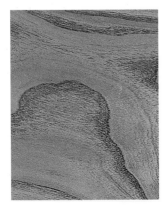

Mulberry

The coloured streaking in ambrosia maple is caused by fungal spores colonizing the tracks left by beetle larvae. This patterning with therefore be erratic, and dependent on how many larvae there are, or how far they move.

The burr figuring in maple is a mixture of swirling grain with striations and small, tight clusters of knots. It cuts satisfactorily, though, just needing the most delicate of shear cuts over the burr formation to get a nice finish.

Quilting usually takes the form of pillow- or cloud-like configurations; others have said that the quilt looks like beads of water on a freshly waxed surface. Whichever description you prefer, the formation is always stunning. Despite the fact that the grain direction in quilted wood is all over the place, it still cuts well as long as you take light cuts with sharp tools.

The rippled maple shown here has a pink tinge to it, with the ripples running across the grain. Some woods take on a pinkish tinge when steamed, beech and pear being two examples. Maple, to my knowledge, is not one of this group, and this aberrant colouring is all natural. It just goes to show that every piece of wood is genuinely different, and when you think you know what's what, nature throws a curve ball just to keep you on your toes.

maple, European *Acer campestre* **Europe**
European or field maple is paler in colour than its American relative, and seems a little denser. The wood is normally a pale cream to buff colour. Being close-grained, maple is often used for kitchen utensils: chopping boards, spatulas and so on. The burr form more often than not comprises tightly packed clusters of small knots. It also is available in large sizes.

mountain laurel *Umbellularia californica* **USA**
This wood ranges in colour from buff to a soft brown, the sapwood being slightly lighter than the heartwood. It has a delicate grain pattern, cuts well and is a delight to turn.

mulberry *Callicarpa americana* **Europe and USA**
A yellow wood with a very pronounced grain pattern. It quickly loses the bright yellow colour, mellowing down to a soft yellow-brown after a week or so. The somewhat open grain structure can be a little tricky to cut with a scraper, but shear-cutting will soon solve this. This is not a commercial timber; it is usually obtained through friends or a friendly local tree surgeon.

Ambrosia maple

Quilted maple

Mountain laurel

oak, European *Quercus robur* **Europe**

European oak is open-grained but dense, and cuts well with all tools. Because of its strength and beauty, and its ability to hold detail without splintering off, it is often used in architectural turning. A deep olive-brown colour, it responds well to oil finishing, acquiring a deep, lustrous shine that is hard to match. The sapwood is just a little paler than the heartwood. Oak is commercially available in large sizes. Quartersawn wood displays some beautiful ray figuring.

The variety known as brown oak is caused by beefsteak fungus, which colours the wood to a deep brown without causing rot. It works as well as the ordinary form and is not discernibly denser.

Holm oak

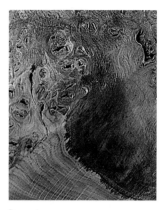

Burr oak

Burr oak often occurs as tight clusters of knots, but can also have swirling grain. The erratic grain structure can be a little tricky to cut cleanly when dry or very old, but if it is turned at about 15% moisture content, there is no problem.

oak, holm *Quercus ilex* **Europe**

Holm or evergreen oak is a deep brown colour, often having black streaks in it. This is a pleasant wood to work with. It has an open grain structure, as do most oaks, but seasons and cuts well. The sap is a cream or buff colour, while the heartwood is a darker brown with the darker streaks. It is not usually commercially available, but is well worth keeping a look-out for.

olive *Olea europaea* **Europe**

This is a wood with a very pronounced grain pattern. It is creamy-buff in colour, with dark brown, black and greenish lines running through it. It is oily – the wet shavings will stain steel and lathe beds – and cuts well, when it has a relatively straight grain. Since olive is a slow-growing tree, it can be somewhat gnarled and may have a slot of swirling, interlocking grain in it. When the wood is like this, it may prove difficult to get a clean cut on it. Take very gentle cuts with a sharp tool, and you should be OK. It is very prone to heat-checking, so use abrasive sparingly, and definitely not aggressively.

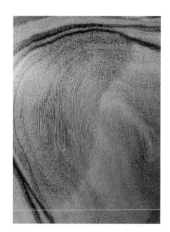

European olive

pear *Pyrus communis* **Europe**

A tight-grained wood that cuts well and has a subtle grain pattern. It is cream in colour, and not prone to substantial colour variations. It cuts well and, while not available in massive sizes, it is ideally suited to hollow forms, small bowls and boxes.

Pear is one of the woods that will turn pink when steamed. This adds another attractive feature to what is already a lovely wood to work with. The steaming does not affect the way it works.

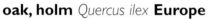

Steamed pear

Pear

London plane

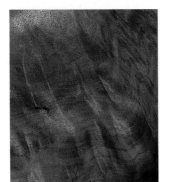

Red morell burr

Rowan

Rose she-oak

plane, London *Platanus acerifolia* **Europe**

A beautiful timber to work with. It cuts well, has a fleck or ray patterning, and responds well to all finishes. Available in large sizes and a variety of thicknesses, it can be used for many of the projects in this book.

poplar, white *Populus* spp. **Europe**

A cream- to buff-coloured wood that can have a somewhat woolly grain. By this I mean that it is a little soft, and can be a bit tricky to finish. Cut lightly with very sharp tools, and expect to have some grain pull-out which can be finished off with abrasive. It is available in large sizes and is prone to forming burrs. The piece shown here has it all: burr, bark inclusions and ripples.

red morell burr
(botanical name uncertain) **Australia**

A red to deep maroon-coloured wood that is dense and has a swirling grain pattern. Even though the grain is so erratic, it cuts well and a very fine finish is achieved straight from the tool.

redwood burr *Sequoia sempervirens* **USA**

A beautiful red to reddish-brown wood that has a lovely grain pattern. It is somewhat softer than a lot of the woods mentioned previously, but cuts well with sharp tools. The burr figuring is erratic: sometimes tight clusters of little knots, other times it can consist of swirling grain around larger knots.

rowan *Sorbus aucuparia* **Europe**

A fine-grained wood that is cream in colour, only available in small sizes, and cuts well. Owing to the small sizes available, it is bought either as a log or part thereof, which means that it is supplied with the bark on. Rowan's bark is small and stays put, so it is ideally suited for use in natural-edged work.

she-oak *Casuarina fraserana* **Australia**

She-oak is a pleasant wood to work with. Not particularly dense, the orange-coloured wood has deeper orange ray flecks running through it when cut, and it cuts well with sharp tools. The orange colour does mellow a little with time, but not by much, so it retains much of the orange hue.

I have to admit to not knowing whether the 'rose' variant is a subspecies or an anomaly, but the colour is a deep red, it cuts and finishes as well as the orange she-oak, and also has the ray flecks when cut.

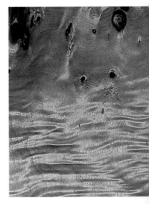

White poplar

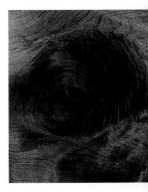

Redwood burr

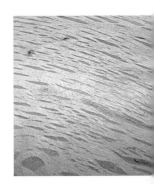

She-oak

sumach *Rhus typhina* **Europe and USA**

The bright, almost iridescent green, yellow and brown colouring of the heartwood never fails to amaze me; the sapwood is a pretty nondescript greyish-cream colour. It has a pronounced grain pattern, is easy to cut and finish, and because of its small size it is ideally suited to hollow forms and boxes. The colour will mellow, but some of the pieces I have made in sumach have retained the majority of their colour even after a couple of years.

sycamore, European
Acer pseudoplatanus **Europe and western Asia**

A close-grained wood that is cream to buff in colour with a subtle grain pattern. It is an absolute gem to work with, cuts well and holds fine detail without splitting off. Available in very large sizes, it is a great wood for all kinds of work. Being close-grained, it is ideally suited for kitchen use.

walnut, European *Juglans regia* **Europe**

The heartwood varies in colour from soft buff to deep brown, with dark streaks running along the grain. The sapwood is of little use: prone to degrade and infection, and an insipid pale cream colour, it is often cut off. Like many other varieties of walnut, it cuts well, is available in a variety of sizes, and it is not uncommon to find burrs or (as here) ripple forms. You are unlikely to find a log that is all burr; these fetch a fortune from veneer makers. Instead, we are more likely to come across small burrs, or pieces with small burr sections in them.

yellow box burr
Eucalyptus melliodora **Australia**

Another eucalypt, this is dense and cuts well becuase of its slightly oily nature. It is close-grained and, as you can see here, the burr form has a few tight knotty areas as well as some swirls.

yew *Taxus baccata* **Europe**

One of my favourite woods. It is dense, slow-growing, often gnarled, full of bark inclusions, has interlocking grain, and is not available in large sections without splits – which often have silica or other mineral deposits in them. Have I put you off yet? It has a rich deep yellow to orange heartwood and a creamy-coloured sapwood. There can be purple patches and streaks in it if iron is present, and if you are prepared to work with it you will be rewarded with a rich patchwork of figuring and colour.

The burr form ranges from swirling grain through to tight clusters of pippy knots. The interlocking grain can be a little tricky to finish, but with sharp tools and a light touch for the finishing cuts, you will be fine. Over-zealous sanding will result in heat-checking, so be gentle with it.

Sumach

European walnut

Yew burr

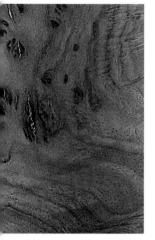

European sycamore

Yellow box burr

Yew

boxes

Boxes are wonderful items and great fun to make. They hint at something secret held inside. Using little wood, they are not expensive to make, require few tools, and offer a vast range of shapes to explore. I believe that all turning skills are best learned, refined and developed on spindle-turned projects like these, and once you have mastered these skills you are well on your way to tackling anything. The adage 'Good things come in little packages' is very true.

6 spice-jar box

page 56

7 ribbed box

page 58

8 finial box

page 60

9 lantern box

page 62

10 pedestal box

page 64

cylindrical box

yellow box
Height: 4⁷⁄₁₆in (113mm)
Diameter: 2⅜in (60mm)

This piece in yellow box is an ideal introduction to the art of making boxes. It is one of the simplest types of box to create, yet it demonstrates the importance of a well-proportioned body and top, a lid that is not too stiff to lift off easily, matching grain throughout the box, nicely detailed lid and base sections, and a fine, lustrous finish.

This project provides an excellent foundation for all the other box designs which follow. The next few pages describe the methods used for all of them: double-mounting (double-chucking) the body and lid; mounting the lid tightly in the base after turning the inside in order to form the final lid profile; then easing the fit, and finally reverse-chucking the base to finish the underside.

A good rule of thumb for creating well-proportioned boxes is to use ⅔ of the height for the base and ⅓ for the lid; an alternative is ⅗ and ⅖. This box is parallel from top to bottom; for a footed box, the foot needs to be at least ⅓ of the overall diameter for the sake of stability.

hints
● **When hollowing the box, mark the gouge with tape to show how far to drill down**
● **Alternatively, use a Forstner bit held in a Jacobs chuck in the tailstock**

This view shows the details of the body–lid joint

tools required
¾in (19mm) spindle roughing gouge
⅜in (10mm) spindle gouge
⅛in (3mm) parting tool
³⁄₃₂in (2mm) parting tool
¼in (6mm) beading and parting tool
¾in (19mm) skew chisel
¾in (19mm) square-end side-cut
    scraper
⅜in (10mm) square-end scraper
Abrasive down to 1500 grit
Danish-style oil

scale: 100%

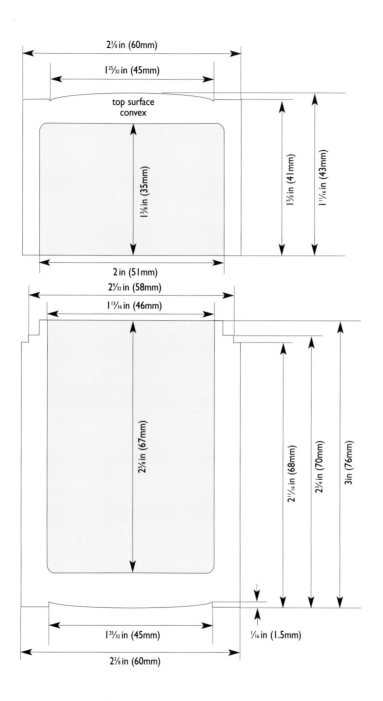

2³⁄₈ in (60mm)

1²⁵⁄₃₂ in (45mm)

top surface
convex

1³⁄₈ in (35mm)

1⁵⁄₈ in (41mm)

1¹¹⁄₁₆ in (43mm)

2 in (51mm)

2⁹⁄₃₂ in (58mm)

1¹³⁄₁₆ in (46mm)

2⁵⁄₈ in (67mm)

2¹¹⁄₁₆ in (68mm)

2³⁄₄ in (70mm)

3 in (76mm)

1²⁵⁄₃₂ in (45mm)

¹⁄₁₆ in (1.5mm)

2³⁄₈ in (60mm)

grain
direction

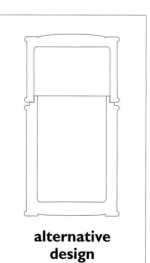

alternative design

The addition of some beads on the side of this design makes it look like a bamboo stem

making the cylindrical box

1 Take a piece of yellow box about 6in long by 2½in square (150 × 63 × 63mm) and mark the diagonals on each end to find the centre

2 Now fix the blank on the lathe between centres. Here it is held between a revolving centre and a four-prong drive held in a chuck. Remember to secure the quill lock on the tailstock so the quill cannot come loose

3 Adjust the rest so that it is about ¼in (6mm) below centre and far enough away not to foul the wood when it is revolved by hand

7 Once the piece is a cylinder, increase the lathe speed to about 1700rpm, take a ⅜in (10mm) beading and parting tool, and clean up the end nearest the tailstock

8 Using the same tool, cut a spigot to fit your chuck. The tool arcs downwards as it cuts

9 Remove the cylinder from between centres and fasten it in your chuck

13 Use the ³⁄₃₂in (2mm) parting tool to part off the lid section from the main body. Part down about ¹⁄₁₆in (1.5mm) in from the lid end of the previous parting cut

14 This will leave a small amount of spigot on each section. Cutting the wood in this manner ensures minimal grain misalignment at the joint

15 Here I am using a ¾in (19mm) skew chisel on its side to refine the spigot. The spigot is parallel to the body and its shoulder is undercut a couple of degrees. If the spigot is not parallel, the lid will not be a nice fit

19 As you get deeper you need to be careful, as the increasing overhang of the gouge can cause some chatter if too big a cut is made

20 With the primary hollowing completed, use a side-cut scraper to clean up the side wall. One or two passes will be enough to make the wall parallel. The wall thickness is about ⁵⁄₁₆in (8mm)

21 Sand and finish the inside. Assuming a good finish from the scraper, you could start sanding at 400 grit. Give the inside a coat of finishing oil and sand it wet, working through the various grades of abrasive down to 1500 grit

4 With the lathe set at about 800rpm, take a ¾in (19mm) spindle roughing gouge and remove the corners of the wood until you have a smooth cylinder

5 Remember that the flute of the gouge always points in the direction of travel, and that many light cuts are better and more controllable than one heavy cut

6 A final pass is made to remove all the bumps

10 Again using the beading and parting tool, clean up and cut a second spigot on the end of the cylinder nearest the tailstock – the end that had the four-prong drive in it

11 With the lathe stopped, measure the length of the cylinder and divide by three. Mark ⅔ of this length up from the chuck end; this part will be the base of the box

12 With a ⅛in (3mm) parting tool, part down no more than 3/16in (5mm) to form the spigot on which the lid will sit. Take another parting cut to the same depth, this time 1/12in (2mm) to one side of the previous cut, making the spigot about 3/16in (5mm) wide

16 The next stage is to hollow out the base. Take a ⅜in (10mm) fingernail-profile spindle gouge and adjust the rest so that when the tool is presented horizontally to the work, it will be on the centre. Present the gouge with its flute facing 10 o'clock, and push it into the revolving wood to bore a central hole

17 Once the centre hole has been bored you can proceed to hollow the box out. The gouge is presented to the work in exactly the same manner, and either traversed from centre to side or arced out from the centre

18 The gouge is now cutting on its lower wing, and it is surprisingly quick to remove the waste

22 Once the finishing is completed, remove the base from the chuck and mount the top

23 Before you cut anything on the lid, measure the diameter of the spigot on the base. This will be slightly less than the original parting-off mark. Transfer this diameter to the lid

24 Using the same boring and hollowing techniques as before, hollow out the inside. Remember not to get too close to the spigot diameter mark

25 As before, use a side-cut scraper to clean up the side wall. Make it parallel and not quite as wide as the spigot diameter mark. We need to create a secure push-fit at this stage, not the suction fit that is our ultimate aim

26 Use a skew chisel on its side to clean up the bottom edge. This will be the meeting face between lid and base, so I undercut it slightly. Now check the base and lid for fit

27 Once you are happy that you have a tight fit, sand and finish the inside and remove the lid from the chuck

31 Using a skew chisel, clean up the cylinder to make it parallel from top to bottom

32 Now that the cylinder is parallel and smooth, take the 3⁄32in (2mm) parting tool and part off the spigot – we will not be mounting it in a chuck again. Back off the tailstock for the final parting off

33 Take the 3⁄8in (10mm) fingernail-profile spindle gouge and make a fine shearing cut from the edge of the lid towards the centre for about 1⁄2in (13mm). If the lid is not a secure fit on the body, it will spin or fly off. If necessary, place a bit of tissue or kitchen towel over the base opening and push the lid on

37 …and the main body with 400 grit, or coarser if there are any blemishes – in which case you will have to work though a few more grades of abrasive later to achieve a good finish

38 I have never known a box to stay perfectly round over time, so, to avoid any unsightly misalignment between base and lid, make a fine cut about 1⁄16in wide and deep (2 x 2mm) just on the base side of the join. This visual break in the profile disguises any movement

39 Now oil the outside of the box …

42 The paper protects the box as you take gentle cuts to remove the spigot. Alternative holding methods are: expanding the chuck and holding on the inside of the cavity; or jam-fitting the work onto a scrap piece of wood, locking on the internal or external profile as necessary

43 The bottom detail is the same as the lid, so the procedures for cutting are the same

44 Oil the bottom …

28 Remount the lid and check the fit again. Here there is a slight gap between the two meeting faces. If this happens, . . .

29 . . . use a skew chisel on its side to undercut the shoulder of the spigot and ensure a good match. If you didn't quite manage to create a secure push-fit, there is a remedy (see step 33), but aim for a secure fit in the first place

30 Now fit the lid, and bring up the tailstock to support it. This technique can be used even when making boxes with finials – just remove the tailstock before the final cuts on the finial

34 Once this section is smooth, take a cut from the centre of the lid out towards the inner section of the cut you have just made. You will need to arc the gouge as you cut towards the edge to create the domed button shape in the centre of the lid. A few passes may be necessary to achieve this profile

35 When satisfied with the shape, you can clean up any surface irregularities with a fine scraping cut. Here, a round-bladed square-end scraper is being held horizontal to the work and rotated so that the edge of the scraper is at 45° to the axial rotation. This is called 'shear-scraping', and allows very fine cuts to be made

36 Now dry-sand the lid . . .

40 . . . and wet-sand through the grades of abrasive as you did on the inside. Remove the lid and sand the spigot to ease the fit a little. The lid should come off gently in the hand when lifted. It only takes a couple of passes; any more, and the fit will become sloppy

41 Once happy with the fit, remove the base from the chuck, place a couple of sheets of kitchen towel over the jaws of the chuck and gently tighten the jaws onto the *open* end of the box

The finished box

45 . . . and sand, working through the various grades to achieve a good finish. Remove from the chuck and fit the two pieces together

2 diabolo box

steamed pear
Height: 5⁷⁄₁₆in (138mm)
Diameter: 2²⁹⁄₃₂in (74mm)

Steamed pear is a wonderful wood to work with. Not only are the subtle pink shades a delight to look at, but it cuts beautifully, so finishing it is a dream.

This project is a logical progression from the straight-sided box, and I think it looks more graceful. I have certainly sold more of them than the straight-sided type, so my customers must agree. The shape resembles the spinning top used in the old-fashioned game of diabolo. If it were scaled down it would look like a stylized chess pawn.

The interior has no sharp corners to collect dirt, which makes cleaning the inside easier, as well as making it nicer to the touch. The curved corners are created with the square-end side-cut scraper, which has a slight radius on the corner cutting edge. This makes light work of the inside walls. As with the first box, the lid and base are double-mounted to maintain grain alignment.

The top has a slight point in the centre, surrounded by a narrow upstanding ring. These details are created after the inside has been turned, jam-fitting the lid onto the base to hold it securely. Once turned, the slight point and ring need to be carefully hand-sanded so as not to lose definition. The fit of the lid is then eased once the shaping is complete. The box is sanded down to 800 grit using lemon oil as a lubricant. A fresh coat of oil is applied, then wiped over with a clean cloth to remove any excess, but on this occasion I decided to leave a matt sheen rather than buffing to a high gloss.

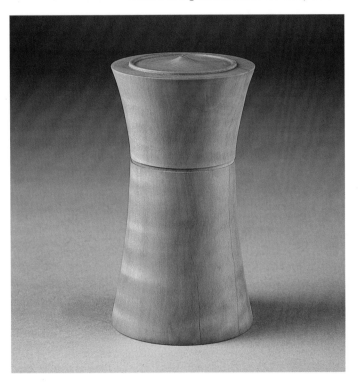

hints
● Form the beads with a ³⁄₃₂in (2mm) fluted parting tool. This will give a perfect bead time and time again
● To save a lot of time removing the waste, pre-bore the box with a Forstner bit in a Jacobs chuck which is held in the tailstock

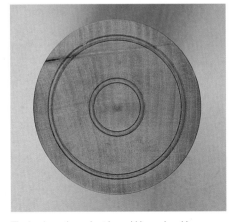

The beads on the underside could be replaced by grooves; the drawing shows one of each

tools used
¾in (19mm) spindle roughing gouge
³⁄₈in (10mm) spindle gouge
⅛in (3mm) parting tool
³⁄₃₂in (2mm) fluted parting tool
¾in (19mm) square-end side-cut scraper with a slight radius on the corner cutting edge
Abrasive down to 800 grit
Lemon oil

scale: 75%
(main drawing)

top detail (enlarged)

³⁄₃₂ in (2mm)

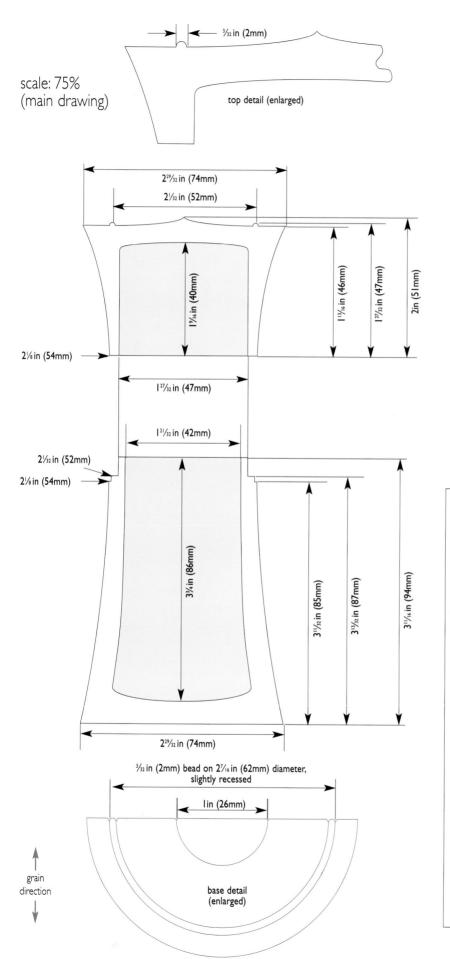

2²⁹⁄₃₂ in (74mm)

2¹⁄₃₂ in (52mm)

1⁹⁄₁₆ in (40mm)

1¹³⁄₁₆ in (46mm)

1²⁷⁄₃₂ in (47mm)

2 in (51mm)

2¹⁄₈ in (54mm)

1²⁷⁄₃₂ in (47mm)

1²¹⁄₃₂ in (42mm)

2¹⁄₃₂ in (52mm)

2¹⁄₈ in (54mm)

3¼ in (86mm)

3¹¹⁄₃₂ in (85mm)

3³⁄₃₂ in (87mm)

3¹¹⁄₁₆ in (94mm)

2²⁹⁄₃₂ in (74mm)

³⁄₃₂ in (2mm) bead on 2⁷⁄₁₆ in (62mm) diameter,
slightly recessed

1 in (26mm)

grain
direction

base detail
(enlarged)

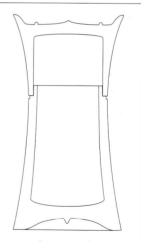

alternative design

This design carries the external walls up higher than the central point to create a castle-like effect. The underside also has a central point, which is a little more aggressive than the top and hints at protective fortifications

3 conical box

rose she-oak
Height: 5in (127mm)
Diameter: 2⅝in (67mm)

The underside is slightly undercut, but has no decoration. This is in keeping with the simple geometric shape

hints
● **Hone the scraper rather than using a bench grinder. You will get a cleaner cut**
● **Wrap the abrasive around a 2 x 1in (50 x 25mm) block of wood to sand the straight outside profile**

I like pyramids and cones, and use the cone shape to make boxes of various sizes. The point of the cone is sharp and can give the impression of danger, but the strong, simple geometric shape is so pleasing that this does not deter people from picking it up.

The dark red colour of the rose she-oak sets the shape off perfectly, as do most other dark woods. Cones made from light-coloured woods tend to look better when they are interspersed with dark ones.

Once again the top and bottom are double-mounted to achieve optimum grain alignment. The cone profile cannot be fully formed until the inside has been turned. Remember to leave enough wood when hollowing to allow a uniform wall thickness throughout.

The most difficult aspect of this box is not the outside profile, but the inside. The internal cavity on the bottom section is finished with a side-cut scraper, but the end

has to be ground back so that it is less than 90° – somewhere about 60° will give you the clearance needed to run the scraper down the side wall and then across the bottom in one uninterrupted movement. Remember to radius off the corner of the scraper. The top internal section is done with a round-nosed side-cut scraper.

A recess is cut where the top and bottom meet, to disguise any misalignment due to shrinkage. Because a cone is not as easy to grip as some shapes, the lid must not be too tight a fit, or it will be difficult to remove. However, it must be tight when first joined back to the base in order to profile the external shape; only after this shaping and sanding can the fit be adjusted by sanding, or by parting a little more wood off the spigot.

The box is dry-sanded and then power-buffed, using a mop loaded with burnishing cream; final buffing is done with a mop loaded with carnauba wax.

If you don't fancy hollowing this type of box, leave the cone solid. Cones make great ornaments or paperweights.

tools used
¾in (19mm) spindle roughing gouge
⅜in (10mm) spindle gouge
⅛in (3mm) parting tool
¾in (19mm) skew chisel
¾in (19mm) modified side-cut scraper with a radius formed on the corner cutting edge.
¾in (19mm) round-nose side-cut scraper
Abrasive down to 800 grit
Power-buffing mop loaded with burnishing cream
Power-buffing mop loaded with carnauba wax

scale: 100%

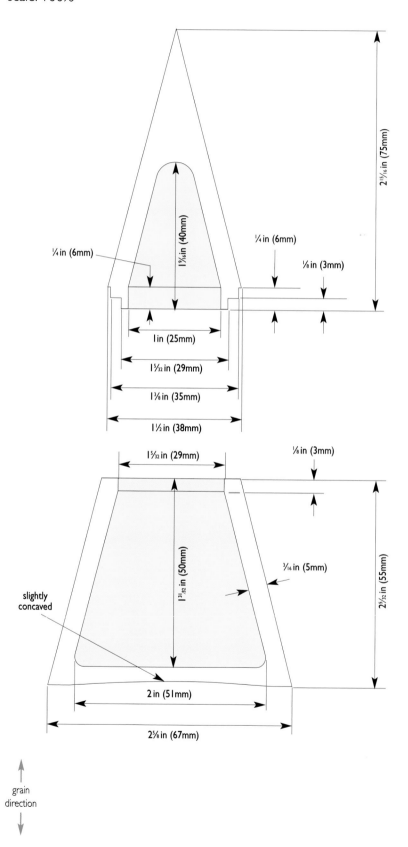

¼ in (6mm)

1⁹⁄₁₆ in (40mm)

¼ in (6mm)

⅛ in (3mm)

2¹⁵⁄₁₆ in (75mm)

1 in (25mm)

1⁵⁄₃₂ in (29mm)

1⅜ in (35mm)

1½ in (38mm)

1⁵⁄₃₂ in (29mm)

⅛ in (3mm)

1³¹⁄₃₂ in (50mm)

³⁄₁₆ in (5mm)

2⁵⁄₃₂ in (55mm)

slightly concaved

2 in (51mm)

2⅝ in (67mm)

grain direction

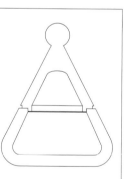

alternative design

A knob at the top of the cone gives a handhold for easier removal of the lid. The bottom profile has also been softened by creating a radius on the lower edge

4 clamshell box

holm oak
Height: 2³⁄₃₂in (53mm)
Diameter: 5¹⁹⁄₃₂in (142mm)

The inspiration for this box came from a clamshell. Rather than carve the ridges, I have opted for a stylized version that makes a nice dressing-table piece. There is no flat on the underside of this box, so it moves when touched, which I think adds to its appeal. The curvaceous profile is great to handle.

The dark striations within the grain of this piece of holm oak create some wonderful patterns which contrast well with the shape. This box has the grain running horizontally, which is unusual for boxes. The blank is bandsawn through the middle, then each half is double-mounted to achieve grain alignment. Because the grain runs crossways – at 90° to the axial rotation of the lathe – we will use bowl-turning tools rather than spindle tools.

The internal curves are all finished off with a shear scraper to minimize the need for coarse grades of abrasive. Once the internal profiles are complete, jumbo plate jaws are used to hold the lid and base in order to finish off the external profile.

The box is sanded with oil as a lubricant, then the inside and outside are power-buffed with a polishing mop loaded with EEE-Ultrashine, followed by power-buffing with a mop loaded with carnauba wax. This is one of the few occasions when I have preferred a shiny surface.

The internal curves match the outside curves. The spigot is not a tight fit; it is there to locate the lid only, not to hold it

hints
● Initially mount the two halves on a screw chuck on the bandsawn face
● Hone the shear scraper, don't just grind it. A suitable presentation angle is 45°, using gentle pressure as you traverse the cutting edge across the surface. The bevel does not rub during the cut

tools used
³⁄₈in (10mm) bowl gouge
⅛in (3mm) parting tool
Shear scraper with a straight and
    a curved face
Abrasive down to 800 grit
Danish oil as a lubricant
Power-buffing mop loaded with EEE-
    Ultrashine
Power-buffing mop loaded with
    carnauba wax

scale: 75%

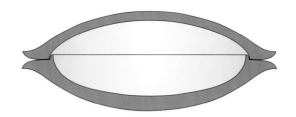

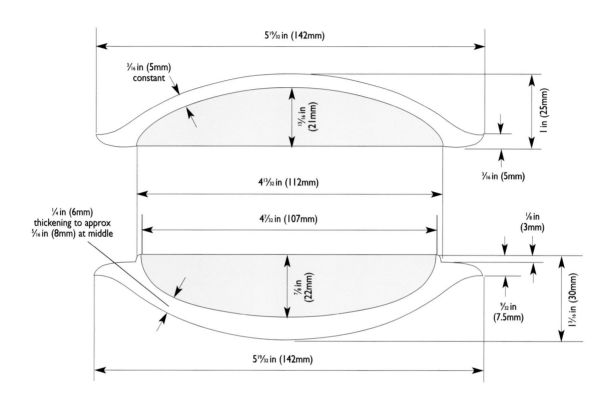

5¹⁹⁄₃₂ in (142mm)

³⁄₁₆ in (5mm)
constant

¹³⁄₁₆ in
(21mm)

1 in (25mm)

³⁄₁₆ in (5mm)

4¹³⁄₃₂ in (112mm)

4⁷⁄₃₂ in (107mm)

¹⁄₄ in (6mm)
thickening to approx
⁵⁄₁₆ in (8mm) at middle

⅛ in
(3mm)

⁷⁄₈ in
(22mm)

⁹⁄₃₂ in
(7.5mm)

1³⁄₁₆ in (30mm)

5¹⁹⁄₃₂ in (142mm)

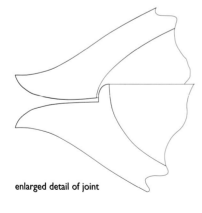

enlarged detail of joint

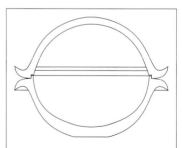

alternative design
This one is more rounded than the main design. It is slightly deeper, so it holds more, and the upturned edge gives the box a Saturn-like appearance

grain
direction

5 perfume-bottle box

A minaret on a mosque and a perfume bottle were the triggers for this design. Its size means that the box is only really useful for storing rings in. However, as with all of the projects in this book, the

laburnum
Height: 3³¹⁄₂in (101mm)
Diameter: 3¹⁄₁₆in (78mm)

sizes can be scaled up or down to suit your requirements. The deep greenish-brown of the laburnum stays that way for a long while. Most other timbers mellow in colour a lot faster than this wood. This piece was made from a small branch section and the pith is just off-centre.

Again the top and bottom are double-mounted. The inside cavity is taken out with a ball-end scraper, and then sanded using paste wax as a lubricant before being wiped over with a clean cloth. This is the only finish on the inside.

The hardest part of this box is the fit of the lid. If the wood is at all wet, the body will move and shrink, in which case the lid will not fit for long. I used a kiln-dried log section, which was stable. There are a few incised V-cuts around the lid and opening to disguise the join. If you find that the lid is a little sloppy when you fit it into the base section for final shaping, place a piece or two of tissue paper in between the lid and base, and push. This should provide the little extra thickness necessary to secure the lid.

The outside is sanded to 600 grit with wax as a lubricant, then oiled; finally the oil is friction-dried at high speed with a clean cloth.

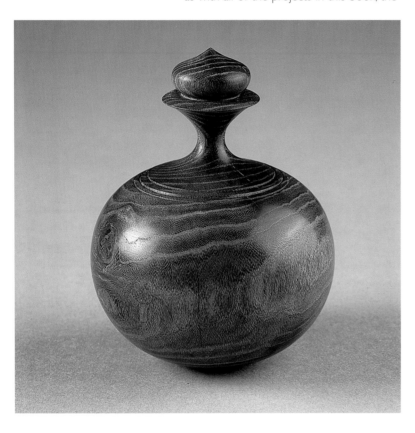

The lid is a gentle push-fit into the main body of the box. The recess for the lid is clearly shown

hints

● **Make the V-cuts with the toe of a skew chisel. This will make a small, cleanly incised cut**
● **Make the lid section where it fits into the body slightly deeper than you need, then clean off the excess as you blend in the curves when the lid and body are fitted together**

tools used

¾in (19mm) spindle roughing gouge
³⁄₈in (10mm) spindle gouge
⅛in (3mm) parting tool
¾in (19mm) ball-end scraper
Abrasive down to 800 grit
Paste wax as a lubricant
Danish oil

scale: 100%

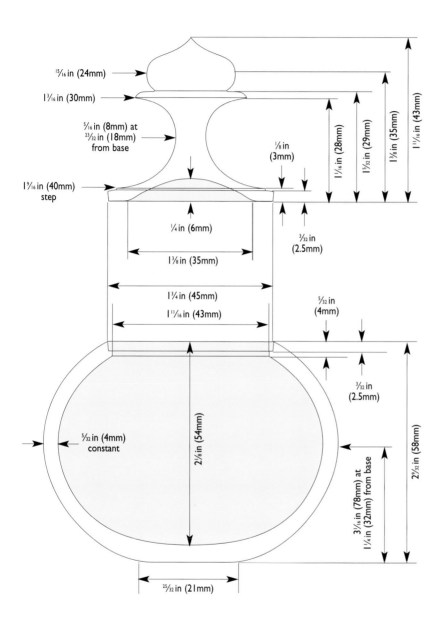

$^{15}/_{16}$ in (24mm)

$1^{3}/_{16}$ in (30mm)

$^{5}/_{16}$ in (8mm) at
$^{23}/_{32}$ in (18mm)
from base

$1^{9}/_{16}$ in (40mm)
step

$^{1}/_{8}$ in
(3mm)

$1^{1}/_{16}$ in (28mm)

$1^{5}/_{32}$ in (29mm)

$1^{3}/_{8}$ in (35mm)

$1^{11}/_{16}$ in (43mm)

$^{1}/_{4}$ in (6mm)

$1^{3}/_{8}$ in (35mm)

$^{3}/_{32}$ in
(2.5mm)

$1^{3}/_{4}$ in (45mm)

$1^{11}/_{16}$ in (43mm)

$^{5}/_{32}$ in
(4mm)

$^{3}/_{32}$ in
(2.5mm)

$^{5}/_{32}$ in (4mm)
constant

$2^{1}/_{8}$ in (54mm)

$2^{9}/_{32}$ in (58mm)

$3^{1}/_{16}$ in (78mm) at
$1^{1}/_{4}$ in (32mm) from base

$^{25}/_{32}$ in (21mm)

grain
direction

**alternative
design**

Some people may prefer the
softened ball top to the
hard-edged finial. The little
pedestal-type foot makes
the box more stable

6 spice-jar box

spalted silver birch
Height: 7¹³⁄₁₆in (198mm)
Diameter: 7in (178mm)

Inspired by a Chinese ginger jar, I felt that spalted wood in some way mimicked the beautiful glaze with which the original jar was decorated. There was no need to add any other form of decoration.

This project, like some of the other boxes, could well be called a 'hollow form'. It is larger than any of the other boxes, but like the others it can be scaled up or down as you require.

Spalted woods can be rather soft. Once the initial shaping was completed, I used cellulose sanding sealer thinned down by 50% to stabilize the wood in readiness for turning it to the required thickness. I coated it about six times with the solution, never letting it dry between coats, to ensure that the fibres became saturated; I left it for two days and then carried on and finished the piece.

The inside is excavated with a hollowing tool which has a 'shield' above the cutting edge to limit the cut. I used a Woodcut Pro-Forme, but a Hamlet Big Brother or an Exocet would have done equally well. The cut limiter provides micro-fine adjustment to allow the most delicate of cuts. This type of tool leaves a very smooth finish that should only require sanding.

The lid is not a tight fit, but is a soft suction fit onto the upstanding spigot. But remember, it's made tight to start with for profiling, then loosened off afterwards.

Both the lid and the body are double-mounted. The curvature of the body is refined with the skew chisel, which gives a very fine, precise cut. I found that the stabilized timber cut well and required very little sanding. The inside and out were sanded down to 600 grit and finished with spray acrylic satin lacquer.

hints
● Keep any excess thinned sanding sealer in a metal or screw-topped glass container to prevent it going off and being wasted
● The tailstock and banjo assembly on a lathe can slip when under pressure. This is usually caused by rubbish, oil, dust and so on, building up on the bed into a compressed, slippery mess under the banjo and tailstock. Once a week, rub some abrasive over the bed and under the banjo and tailstock units to keep them clean. While you are doing this, it is also worth rubbing the abrasive over the rest a couple of times to keep this clean and free of nicks

The radiused inside edge of the spigot on the main body is gentle on the hand when you reach in for some cookies

tools used
¾in (19mm) spindle roughing gouge
⅜in (10mm) spindle gouge
⅛in (3mm) parting tool
¾in (19mm) skew chisel
¾in (19mm) round-nosed scraper
'Shielded' hollowing tool
Sanding stick with a ball end on which abrasive is held.
Abrasive down to 600 grit
Acrylic satin lacquer spray

scale: 60%

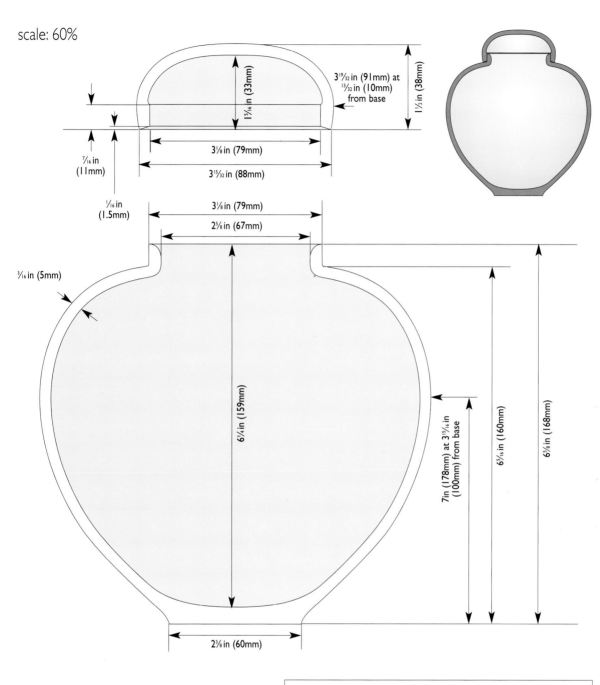

$3^{19}/_{32}$ in (91mm) at $^{13}/_{32}$ in (10mm) from base

$1^{1}/_{2}$ in (38mm)

$1^{5}/_{16}$ in (33mm)

$3^{1}/_{8}$ in (79mm)

$3^{15}/_{32}$ in (88mm)

$^{7}/_{16}$ in (11mm)

$^{1}/_{16}$ in (1.5mm)

$3^{1}/_{8}$ in (79mm)

$2^{5}/_{8}$ in (67mm)

$^{3}/_{16}$ in (5mm)

$6^{1}/_{4}$ in (159mm)

7in (178mm) at $3^{15}/_{16}$ in (100mm) from base

$6^{5}/_{16}$ in (160mm)

$6^{5}/_{8}$ in (168mm)

$2^{3}/_{8}$ in (60mm)

grain direction

alternative design

This is another style of ginger jar. There is a ball finial at the top to lift the lid, and a foot to make the box 'float' off the surface on which it stands

7 ribbed box

boxwood
Length: 5⅞in (149.5mm)
Diameter: 2¾in (70mm)

The shape of this box is based on an American football, but, as you can see, it has been somewhat elongated.

Boxwood is a beautiful wood to work with. It is dense and cuts cleanly. This piece is slightly spalted, which gives an added

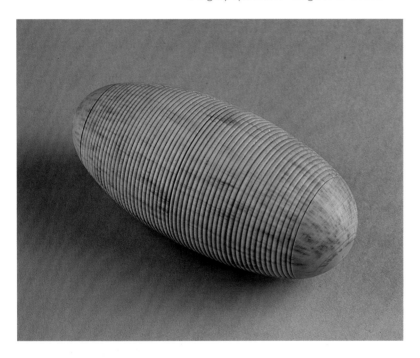

The inside is smooth and silky to the touch, as are the ends of the box, forming an effective contrast to the beads. The spigot can be seen clearly in this view

dimension to the box. Much of the surface is covered with a series of ³⁄₃₂in (2mm) beads, which add a contrasting texture to the smooth curves. Fine beads are only successful if the wood is dense enough for them to be cut cleanly; boxwood is a great choice.

As you have now come to expect, the lid and base are double-mounted to ensure grain alignment. Base and lid of this box are each exactly half the overall length, excluding the spigot. There is no flattened foot area, so the box is free to roll on a dressing table or other surface, but is a delight to touch. The lid is fitted tightly while the profiling is being carried out, but eased off afterwards to form a suction fit, so it stays in place until pulled apart. The box can hold quite a bit – a ring and a couple of necklaces, maybe.

The inside curves are formed with a French-curve scraper, and then sanded using paste wax as a lubricant.

Once the inside is complete, the external profile is completed and sanded before the beads are cut with a ³⁄₃₂in (2mm) fluted parting tool.

After dry-sanding down to 600 grit, the box is finished with lemon oil. The matt lustre brings out the beauty in the wood.

hints
● The beads are formed with the fluted parting tool. To ensure uniformly spaced beads, place one of the wing tips of the tool in the previous groove as you make the cut
● Provided the fluted parting tool is kept nice and sharp-cutting, it should produce crisply delineated beads requiring only minimal sanding with fine abrasive

tools used
¾in (19mm) spindle roughing gouge
⅜in (10mm) spindle gouge
⅛in (3mm) parting tool
³⁄₃₂in (2mm) fluted parting tool
¾in (19mm) skew chisel
¾in (19mm) round-nosed scraper
Abrasive down to 600 grit
Lemon oil

scale: 75%

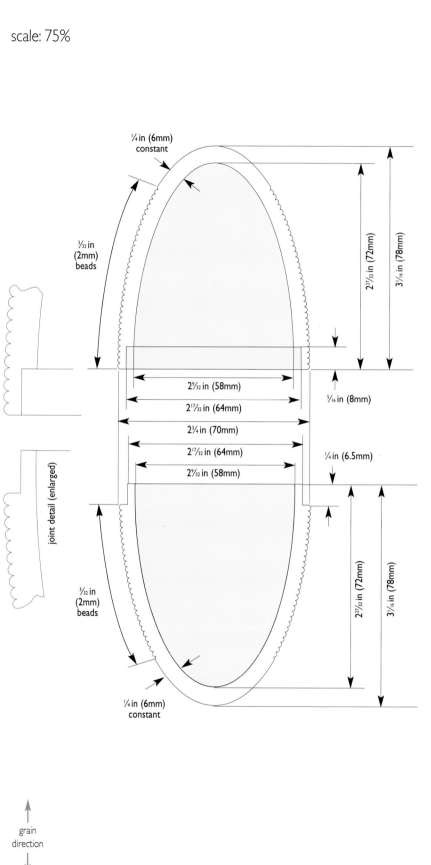

¼ in (6mm) constant

³⁄₃₂ in (2mm) beads

joint detail (enlarged)

$2^{27}/_{32}$ in (72mm)

$3^{1}/_{16}$ in (78mm)

$2^{9}/_{32}$ in (58mm)

$2^{17}/_{32}$ in (64mm)

$2^{3}/_{4}$ in (70mm)

$2^{17}/_{32}$ in (64mm)

$2^{9}/_{32}$ in (58mm)

$5/_{16}$ in (8mm)

¼ in (6.5mm)

³⁄₃₂ in (2mm) beads

¼ in (6mm) constant

$2^{27}/_{32}$ in (72mm)

$3^{1}/_{16}$ in (78mm)

grain direction

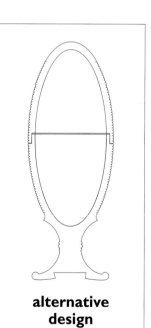

alternative design

An elongated egg in an eggcup is the theme for this variant. The beads are the same, but this time the box is upended and has a pedestal foot

8 finial box

olive

Height: 5⅜in (136mm)
Diameter: 2⅞in (73mm)

Olive is a beautiful timber to work with, and its 'marbled' appearance is particularly effective on this project. However, its erratic grain direction can cause a few problems on the thin stem of the finial. The bulbous body is pleasing to the touch, while the finial, as well as looking good, also provides a convenient

hints

● **To help resist rotational forces, keep the widest part of the blade of the scraper in contact with the rest, and not the reduced section of the shank**
● **When you need to knock a lathe centre into a piece of wood to secure it properly, use a wooden or urethane mallet to avoid damage. A metal hammer would soon burr over and deform the Morse taper, which would prevent accurate seating in the tailstock and headstock tapers**

Many people will decorate the underside of the lid, but often the foot is neglected. I think that all parts of a piece should be thought about and finished to the same standard. There is a recessed button-like dome in the foot of this box

handhold with which to lift the inset lid. But do make sure that the lid is not a tight-fitting one, or there may be a risk of breaking off the finial.

This box does not follow the conventional rules of lid-to-body ratio, such as 1 : 2 or 2 : 3 – but these rules are only a guide in any case. I often find that finial boxes work better if they do not follow the rules too slavishly.

Both the lid and the body have to be chucked twice, as described for the cylindrical box on pages 44–7. This lid is not held in the body for final shaping. Instead, hold it on its outside rim, in a chuck whose jaws are padded with tissue paper to prevent marring.

When turning the finial, it is essential to form the end of the finial first – in this case the small minaret top – and then work back in stages towards the chuck. This will minimize flexing of the workpiece, thus reducing the risk of breaking the stem.

The box is sanded down to 1200 grit, using paste wax as a lubricant to minimize heat. The outside is then finished off with lemon oil, which is finally power-buffed using a polishing mop loaded with burnishing cream.

tools used

¾in (19mm) spindle roughing gouge
⅜in (10mm) spindle gouge
⅛in (3mm) parting tool
¾in (19mm) skew chisel
¾in (19mm) round side-cut scraper
Abrasive down to 1200 grit
Paste wax as a lubricant
Lemon oil
Power-buffing mop loaded with
   EEE-Ultrashine

scale: 100%

¼ in (6.5mm)

⁹⁄₃₂ in (7mm)

⅛ in (3.5mm)
at 2⁵⁄₃₂ in (58mm)
from base

¾ in (19mm)

⁷⁄₁₆ in (11mm)

1¼ in (32mm)

¼ in (6.5mm)

2¹⁹⁄₃₂ in (66mm)

2¹¹⁄₁₆ in (68mm)

2⅞ in (73mm) o/a

3¹⁄₃₂ in (25mm)

1⅛ in (28mm)

1¹⁄₁₆ in (27mm)

1¼ in (32mm)

1½ in (38mm)

¹¹⁄₁₆ in (8mm)

⅛ in (3mm)

¼ in (6.5mm)

³⁄₁₆ in (5mm)

³⁄₃₂ in (2mm)

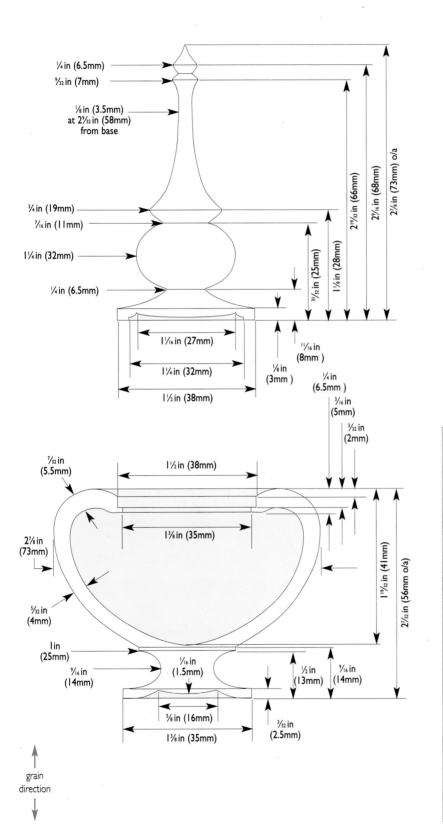

⁷⁄₃₂ in (5.5mm)

1½ in (38mm)

2⅞ in (73mm)

1⅜ in (35mm)

⁵⁄₃₂ in (4mm)

1 in (25mm)

⁹⁄₁₆ in (14mm)

¹⁄₁₆ in (1.5mm)

1¹⁹⁄₃₂ in (41mm)

2¹⁄₃₂ in (56mm o/a)

½ in (13mm)

⁹⁄₁₆ in (14mm)

⅝ in (16mm)

³⁄₃₂ in (2.5mm)

1⅜ in (35mm)

grain
direction

alternative design

If the original finial is not to your taste, modify it. By adding a small bead around the rim of the foot, the shape of the foot is 'softened' to match the curved body

9 lantern box

cypress
Height: 9³⁄₁₆in (233mm)
Width: 3in (76mm)

Square edges can add an interesting dimension to a turning. In this case I have created a tall box with square base and lid sections and a finial. The lid and base are double-mounted.

The most difficult aspect of this box is obtaining the clean, square corners. This is achieved by setting off the section to be cut by means of an incising cut with the skew chisel, prior to making the ordinary parting cut with a parting tool.

The main body cavity is bored with a Forstner bit held in a Jacobs chuck in the tailstock, then finished off with a side-cut scraper. The inside of the lid is finished with a round-nose scraper, but care must be taken not to damage the square side-wall section that provides the meeting face for the spigot.

As usual, the fit between lid and body is made tight at first in order to profile the lid and finial, then eased off a little once the profile is complete.

The whole piece is dry-sanded down to 600 grit, then finished with lemon oil.

The underside of the lid is domed within the spigot recess

hints
● **Practise cutting the square edges on a scrap piece of wood beforehand – pine is a good choice. If you can cut pine cleanly, then other woods are easy in comparison**
● **Always start from the end of the finial nearest the tailstock, working back to the main lid section. This will minimize vibration and the risk of snapping the stem**

tools used
¾in (19mm) spindle roughing gouge
⅜in (10mm) spindle gouge
⅛in (3mm) parting tool
¾in (19mm) skew chisel
¾in (19mm) square-end side-cut
    scraper with a slight radius on the
    corner cutting edge
¾in (19mm) round-nose scraper
Abrasive down to 600 grit
Lemon oil

scale: 60%

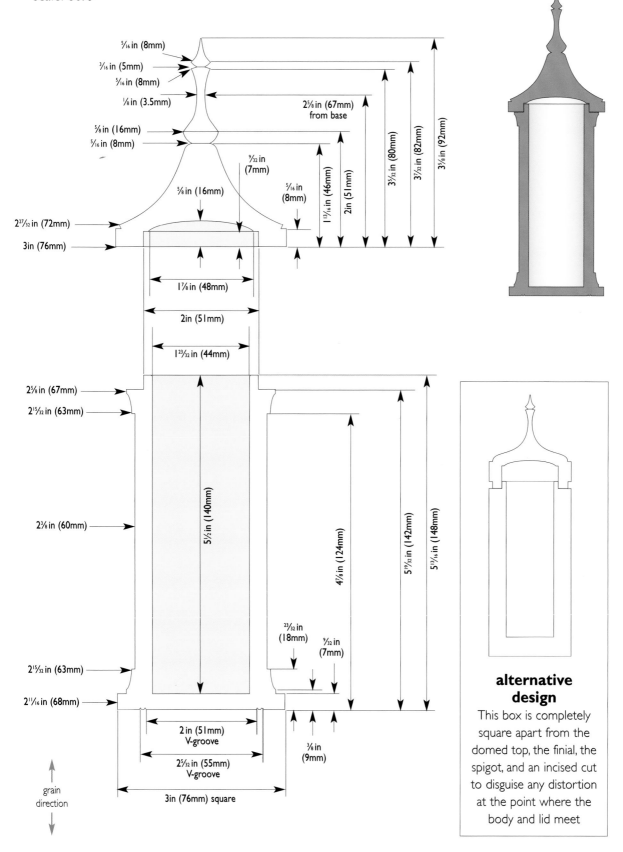

⁵⁄₁₆ in (8mm)

³⁄₁₆ in (5mm)

⁵⁄₁₆ in (8mm)

⅛ in (3.5mm)

2⅝ in (67mm) from base

⅝ in (16mm)

⁵⁄₁₆ in (8mm)

⅝ in (16mm)

⁹⁄₃₂ in (7mm)

⁵⁄₁₆ in (8mm)

3⁵⁄₃₂ in (80mm)

3⁷⁄₃₂ in (82mm)

3⅝ in (92mm)

1¹³⁄₁₆ in (46mm)

2 in (51mm)

2²⁷⁄₃₂ in (72mm)

3 in (76mm)

1⅞ in (48mm)

2 in (51mm)

1²³⁄₃₂ in (44mm)

2⅝ in (67mm)

2¹⁵⁄₃₂ in (63mm)

2⅜ in (60mm)

5½ in (140mm)

4⅞ in (124mm)

5¹⁹⁄₃₂ in (142mm)

5¹³⁄₁₆ in (148mm)

2¹⁵⁄₃₂ in (63mm)

2¹¹⁄₁₆ in (68mm)

²³⁄₃₂ in (18mm)

⁹⁄₃₂ in (7mm)

2 in (51mm) V-groove

2⁵⁄₃₂ in (55mm) V-groove

⅜ in (9mm)

3 in (76mm) square

grain direction

alternative design

This box is completely square apart from the domed top, the finial, the spigot, and an incised cut to disguise any distortion at the point where the body and lid meet

10 pedestal box

beech burr
Height: 7¾in (197mm)
Diameter: 2¼in (57mm)

A pedestal box with a delicate finial is the last project in this section. Close inspection reveals that the box is slightly narrower at the join of the lid than at the bottom of the main body section. This tapering, I thought, looked better than a parallel body section. If you don't agree, you can make the main body parallel.

The mottling on the beech burr looks fantastic. The fascinating thing about burrs is that no two pieces are identical. The irregular pink colouring on this piece is also unique. The other section of beech burr that I have is only a mottled brown.

Without meaning to sound repetitive, the body and lid are double-mounted. The lid is a gentle suction fit – too tight, and you may snap off the finial when trying to remove the lid. The lid was held in jaws lined with tissue paper to prevent marring while turning the finial section.

The inside and out were dry-sanded down to 600 grit, then finished with spray satin acrylic lacquer.

The underside of the lid shows the simple domed shape; the spigot is on the lid this time

hints
● **Apply aerosol acrylic-based lacquer outdoors –** the smell is awful, and permeates through the house if the workshop is annexed to it. Even if you work in a shed, it's still a smell that you do not want to suffer with too long
● **Fold your abrasive in half to create a sharp edge with which to sand the finial.**

tools used
¾in (19mm) spindle roughing gouge
⅜in (10mm) spindle gouge
⅛in (3mm) parting tool
¾in (19mm) skew chisel
¾in (19mm) round-nose side-cut scraper
Abrasive down to 600 grit
Spray satin acrylic lacquer

scale: 75%

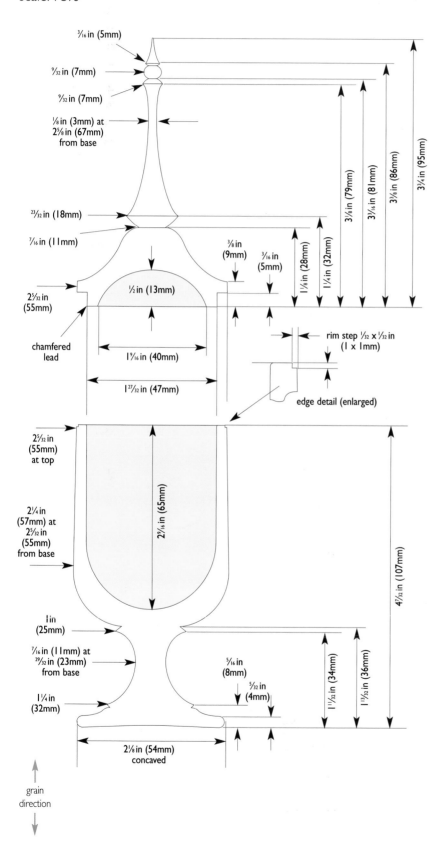

³⁄₁₆ in (5mm)

⁹⁄₃₂ in (7mm)

⁹⁄₃₂ in (7mm)

⅛ in (3mm) at
2⅝ in (67mm)
from base

3¼ in (95mm)

3⅜ in (86mm)

3³⁄₁₆ in (81mm)

3⅛ in (79mm)

²³⁄₃₂ in (18mm)

⁷⁄₁₆ in (11mm)

⅜ in (9mm)

³⁄₁₆ in (5mm)

1¼ in (32mm)

1⅛ in (28mm)

2⁵⁄₃₂ in (55mm)

chamfered lead

½ in (13mm)

1⁹⁄₁₆ in (40mm)

1²⁷⁄₃₂ in (47mm)

rim step ¹⁄₃₂ x ¹⁄₃₂ in (1 x 1mm)

edge detail (enlarged)

2⁵⁄₃₂ in (55mm) at top

2¼ in (57mm) at 2⁵⁄₃₂ in (55mm) from base

2⁹⁄₁₆ in (65mm)

1 in (25mm)

⁷⁄₁₆ in (11mm) at ²⁹⁄₃₂ in (23mm) from base

1¼ in (32mm)

⁵⁄₁₆ in (8mm)

⁵⁄₃₂ in (4mm)

1¹¹⁄₃₂ in (34mm)

1¹³⁄₃₂ in (36mm)

4²⁄₃₂ in (107mm)

2⅛ in (54mm) concaved

grain direction

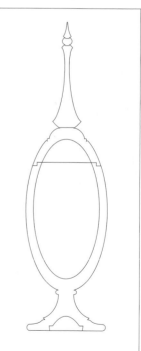

alternative design

Details from the pedestal box are here combined with the elongated oval shape used for the ribbed box (pages 58–9)

bowls

1 fruit
bowl

2 rice
bowl

3 ogee
bowl

4 bowl with
rolled rim

5 bowl with
incurved
rim

Bowls are probably one of the first things people make as they start out on the journey that is woodturning. However, it doesn't take long before one realizes that there are very few actual shapes that have to be learned – it is the combination of shape, proportion and finish that will determine whether the bowl 'works' or not. Some strive to achieve the perfect form or shape all their lives, others enjoy the challenge of creating something new or pushing themselves a little further with a finer cut here, a thinner wall there, and so on. Whether you plan to produce functional bowls, or ones that will be admired and displayed in a cabinet, turning bowls will allow you to develop your skills quickly and have fun doing so.

6 round-bottom bowl

7 deep bowl

8 flared bowl

9 square bowl

10 winged bowl

page 82

page 84

page 86

page 88

page 90

fruit bowl

white poplar burr
Height: 2⁹⁄₁₆in (65mm)
Diameter: 12¹⁹⁄₃₂in (320mm)

White poplar is a beautiful wood to work with. This design shows off the figure in the grain well, and makes an attractive bowl that can be used to store fruit, pot-pourri and other such items. It is not too big, so the wood for it will not cost the earth. It has a raised foot that is attractively detailed underneath, and the outside of the foot curves in the opposite direction to the main sweeping external curve, forming an ogee. The domed rim has an incurving wall that will hold items nicely and throw a crisp shadow around the rim area.

This piece of white poplar burr has some fantastic figuring that really shimmers once oiled. The full extent of the figuring was not evident until the piece had been partially turned. There was a hint of something special in the blank that blossomed as I worked on it. It is this process of exploration and anticipation that makes turning such fun.

The methods described for this project are used for all the bowls in the book. The blank is first mounted on a screw chuck for turning the outside to completion, then reversed and remounted in a four-jaw chuck, using either a spigot or a recess. Once the inside is finished, the piece is reverse-chucked to finish the foot.

The simplicity of this shallow bowl sets off the spectacular shimmering figure of the poplar burr

hints
● Make the width of the foot between ⅓ and ½ of the overall diameter. This will make a stable bowl – any less, and it will look as though it is going to topple. Some bowls have a narrow foot and look stunning, but these are strictly ornaments rather than functional pieces
● It is best to use a slow speed when sanding, to allow the abrasive to cut

tools used
⅜in (10mm) fingernail-profile bowl
   gouge with 45° bevel
⅜in (10mm) square-ground bowl
   gouge with 60° bevel
⅜in (10mm) spindle gouge
⅛in (3mm) parting tool
Tipped shear scraper
¾in (19mm) square-end scraper
Abrasive down to 400 grit
Interior finishing oil
Power-buffing mop loaded with
   burnishing cream

scale: 60%

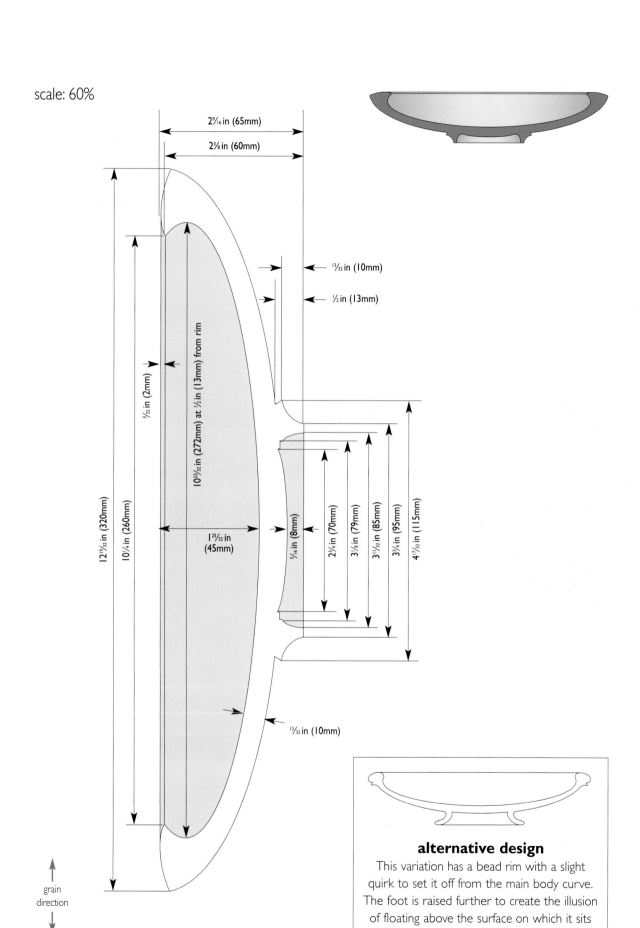

2⁵⁄₁₆ in (65mm)

2³⁄₈ in (60mm)

¹³⁄₃₂ in (10mm)

½ in (13mm)

³⁄₃₂ in (2mm)

10²³⁄₃₂ in (272mm) at ½ in (13mm) from rim

12¹⁹⁄₃₂ in (320mm)

10¼ in (260mm)

1²⁵⁄₃₂ in (45mm)

⁵⁄₁₆ in (8mm)

2¾ in (70mm)

3⅛ in (79mm)

3¹¹⁄₃₂ in (85mm)

3¾ in (95mm)

4¹⁷⁄₃₂ in (115mm)

¹³⁄₃₂ in (10mm)

grain
direction

alternative design
This variation has a bead rim with a slight
quirk to set it off from the main body curve.
The foot is raised further to create the illusion
of floating above the surface on which it sits

making the fruit bowl

1 The blank is 13in (330mm) across by 3in (75mm) thick. Find the centre and drill a hole to suit your screw chuck. This chuck has holes in the flange to take a few screws for extra security

2 Once the screw chuck is secure, mount it on the lathe. The side with the screw chuck in it will be excavated to form the inside of the bowl

3 Place the toolrest assembly parallel to the face of the bowl and adjust the rest so that it is about ¼in (6mm) below centre . . .

4 . . . and far enough away not to foul the blank when it is revolved by hand

8 The odd push cut will be needed to clean up the outer edge

9 At this stage do not worry about the finish on the wood; concentrate on the profile

10 There is still a large deformity on the edge, so a few more cuts are needed. The beginnings of the foot are visible at this stage

11 As you approach the required shape, make a delicate push cut to clean up the surface and remove some of the blemishes

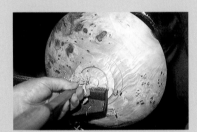

16 I will be using serrated jaws, so require a parallel bore to locate them in. A ¾in (19mm) square-end scraper is used to clean out the recess. Instead of making the bottom flat, I chose to create a shallow dome

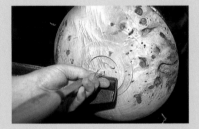

17 This could have been cut with a bowl gouge, but a scraper is just as effective. Once the dome is made, one final cut with the parting tool cleans up the side walls and creates a slight flat to delineate the dome from the side wall and allow the top of the jaws to seat on a square face

18 One final cut with a scraper cleans up the base. It is slightly undercut, to ensure that the maximum width of the foot will sit on the table

22 Moisten the wood with water (do not soak it – no water must get on electric parts) and wet-sand at 500 rpm. Apply a coat of finishing oil over the bowl . . .

23 . . . then either hand-sand or power-sand down to 400 grit. If you find this creates dust, stop the lathe and apply more oil. Carry on working through the grades of abrasive

24 Once sanded, apply the final coat of oil . . .

25 . . . and buff, wiping off the excess after 5 minutes or so with kitchen paper

5 With the lathe set at about 600rpm, take a ⅜in (10mm) fingernail-profile gouge and, starting from the centre, make a pulling cut towards the outer edge. The bevel is rubbing throughout this cut. Make a few passes to remove all the bumps. This will be the underside of the bowl

6 Once the surface is free of undulations, make a push cut at a 45° angle across the edge of the blank to remove some of the unevenness. Note that the flute always points in the direction of travel, and many light cuts (⅛–¼in/3–6mm deep) are more controllable than one heavy cut

7 Once this cut is made, revert to the pull cut and start profiling the external curve of the bowl. Large, aggressive, curved sweeping cuts are made from about 5in (125mm) from the centre toward the outside edge

12 Use a bowl gouge to undercut the foot area slightly. The foot on this bowl is about 5in (125mm) wide

13 Now speed up the lathe to about 1100rpm. With the fingernail gouge, incise a line to delineate the recurved foot, then make a push cut from this point towards the outer edge

14 Use a screwdriver or an awl to pick out any bark inclusions that might become loose during turning. It is better to remove them now than have them fly out at high speed later

15 Using a ⅛in (3mm) parting tool, make a parting cut ¼in (6mm) deep at the required diameter to suit your chuck jaws

19 With the parting tool, clean up the shoulder that sets off the base curve from the main body

20 This tipped shear scraper has different curves and flats on it that can be brought into play by rotating the tip as necessary. The square face is used here, tilted at 45° and pulled across the surface. The rounded shank means that the cut is always supported; if you tilted a rectangular blade to this angle, the cut would be unsupported and might catch

21 The bevel does not rub during the shear cut. The angle of approach can be varied: if you find you are tearing the wood, adjust the angle until you achieve a fine peeling cut. The aim is to clean up the surface of the bowl and minimize the need for sanding with coarse grades

26 Mount a power-buffing mop in a drill, or in a Jacobs chuck on the lathe, and load it with burnishing cream or a fine abrasive compound such as Diamond White

27 Buff the bowl with the lathe running at about 1000rpm. The mop should run in contra-rotation to the work, and be traversed across the surface in an even manner, never stopping in one place for too long. This will leave a beautiful, lustrous satin finish

28 The final stage on the outside is to wipe over the surface with a clean cloth to remove any residue

29 The cloth has picked up all of the buffing residue. With the underside complete, the bowl can be removed from the screw chuck

30 Remount it onto the jaws that fit in the recess cut in the bottom of the bowl. Make sure that the chuck is done up tightly, but not tightly enough to break the wall of the foot

31 Place the toolrest parallel to the face of the bowl, about ¼in (6mm) below centre and far enough away from the wood. Make a push cut from the outer edge towards the centre with a ⅜in (10mm) square-ground bowl gouge. You can use the fingernail gouge, but I find that on the internal curves of bowls I get a sweeter cut with the square-ground gouge. The speed is between 1000 and 1400 rpm

35 The rim is slightly undercut to create the recurve. Do this with the fingernail-profile gouge, which will give you access, then revert to the square-ground gouge

36 The small dome or pyramid of wood left in the centre must now be removed with a few light push cuts

37 Now take a few finishing cuts running from the rim area down to the centre. Traverse the gouge gently across the curvature, making fine cuts to minimize and remove any grain tear-out

42 If the abrasive becomes clogged, use a suede brush to clean it off

43 Work through all of the grades to 400 grit

44 Once sanded, apply another coat of oil

45 Wipe over with a clean cloth

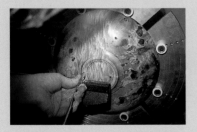

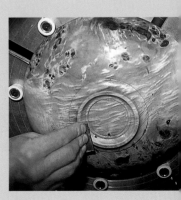

49 Using a spindle gouge, form a small cove on the foot to remove the chucking marks and then create an in-sweep that leads the eye to the central dome

50 Oil and wet-sand once the cove is finished . . .

51 . . . apply a final coat of oil . . .

52 . . . and buff to the same finish as the rest of the bowl

32 Make as many cuts as necessary until the face of the bowl is flat, then form the rim by making an arcing cut towards the outside, starting about 1¼in (30mm) in from the edge

33 Now start to hollow out the centre by making many scooping cuts from the face into the middle, . . .

34 . . . gradually working back towards to the outer edge

38 Adjust the tipped shear scraper so that the longest curved edge is presented to the work at a 45° angle, then make a shear cut on the internal curve of the bowl. We are going against the grain here, but it is such a gentle peeling cut that this makes little difference

39 Redefine the rim with the fingernail-profile gouge . . .

40 . . . then shear-scrape the rim, using the flat face of the shear scraper

41 Once satisfied with the surface finish, apply a coat of oil with the lathe stationary, then wet-sand with the lathe running, as before

46 Power-buff with the mop loaded with burnishing cream . . .

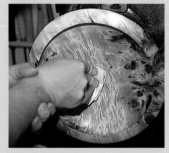

47 . . . and wipe over with a clean cloth or kitchen paper to remove the residue

48 Mount the bowl flat on the jumbo jaws and tighten the plates so that the bowl is gripped by the non-marring rubber bungs. Alternatively, use the friction-drive technique shown on page 27

The finished fruit bowl

2 rice bowl

olive ash
Height: 2⅟₁₆in (65mm)
Diameter: 8⁹⁄₃₂in (210mm)

A footed bowl with a gentle sweeping curve is one of those projects that look easy to make, but any deviations in the curvature are immediately visible and will spoil the look. This piece, modelled on a Japanese rice bowl, is functional, but is also elegant enough to command space of its own and be admired. The walls are thin, so the finished piece is very light. The olive and brown colouring in the wood does not distract the eye from the form. The foot has a small bead on the outside at the junction with the body, which is large enough to notice, but not so large as to jump out and dominate this area. If you prefer to leave the intersection clean, you do not have to use the bead.

The bowl is mounted on a screw chuck while the back is turned. Once turned, sanded and finished, it is reversed and the foot held in the jaws of a chuck for turning the inside. The foot is not undercut at this stage, but left solid to provide a secure mounting. After the inside has been turned and finished, the bowl is reverse-chucked so the foot can be shaped; foot details are shown below, left.

Because it has areas of dark colouring, this bowl was dry-sanded; wet sanding would have risked colour contamination from the oil and dust slurry.

A bowl of this shape may be used for holding food, so it is sensible to use a food-safe finish. In this case I used Hard Burnishing Oil, wiped on with kitchen paper while the lathe was stopped, and then burnished with the lathe running. This created a satin finish which complements the colouring of the wood.

This view of the underside shows how the internal section of the foot follows the same curvature as the main body. Once the main part is complete, the bowl is gripped in jumbo jaws while this section and the external face of the foot are turned

hints
● **Hone rather than grind the tip of the shear scraper. Not only do you achieve a finer cutting edge, but you also save money. Grinding wastes steel, and should be reserved for re-profiling or repairing a damaged edge**
● **Remember when hand-sanding to keep the abrasive moving at all times, to avoid creating sanding rings**

tools used
⅜in (10mm) fingernail-profile bowl gouge
⅜in (10mm) square-ground bowl gouge
⅛in (3mm) parting tool
³⁄₃₂in (2mm) fluted parting tool
Tipped shear scraper
Abrasive down to 600 grit
Organoil Hard Burnishing Oil

scale: 75%

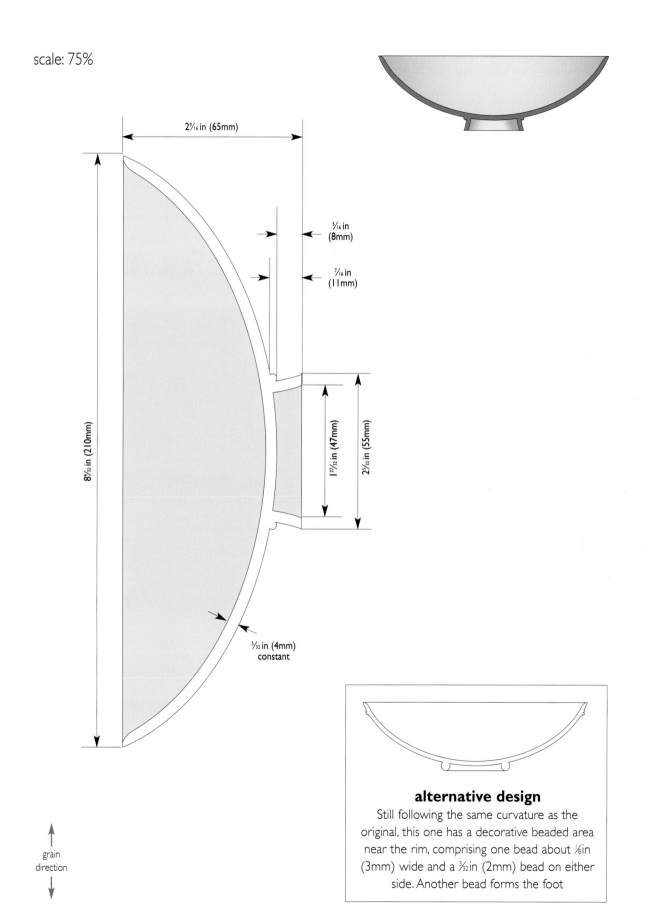

2⁵⁄₁₆ in (65mm)

⁵⁄₁₆ in (8mm)

⁷⁄₁₆ in (11mm)

8⁷⁄₃₂ in (210mm)

1²⁷⁄₃₂ in (47mm)

2³⁄₃₂ in (55mm)

⁵⁄₃₂ in (4mm) constant

grain direction

alternative design
Still following the same curvature as the original, this one has a decorative beaded area near the rim, comprising one bead about ⅛ in (3mm) wide and a ³⁄₃₂ in (2mm) bead on either side. Another bead forms the foot

3 ogee bowl

london plane
Height: 2$^{7}/_{32}$in (56mm)
Diameter: 8$^{11}/_{32}$in (220mm)

An ogee is the form chosen for this bowl. This is a classic profile, though the form can be squashed, made taller or stretched as you desire. The speckled appearance of quartersawn London plane is shown to its fullest with this profile.

The procedure for making this is the same as for the previous bowl, but we are creating an ogee here in place of the sweeping curve. Note how the edge of the rim is softened. The outer edge is rolled over slightly by rubbing some abrasive over the rim while the lathe is rotating. This removes the sharp edge formed during turning and makes it pleasant to handle.

The bowl is wet-sanded down to 600 grit, using Danish oil as the lubricant. It is then power-buffed.

This bowl uses the same foot design as the previous project, and is finished in the same way. It provides an ideal area for signing your work; I do this with a pyrograph unit

hints
● When power-sanding, keep the pad moving across the surface of the work. If you do not, you may sand hollows in the work and ruin the curvature
● The bead can be formed in many ways: with a gouge or a parting tool, or with a special bead-forming tool, available from a number of manufacturers

tools used
$^{3}/_{8}$in (10mm) fingernail-profile bowl gouge
$^{3}/_{8}$in (10mm) square-ground bowl gouge
$^{1}/_{8}$in (3mm) parting tool
$^{3}/_{32}$in (2mm) fluted parting tool
Tipped shear scraper
Abrasive down to 600 grit
Power-buffing mop loaded with EEE-Ultrashine
Danish oil

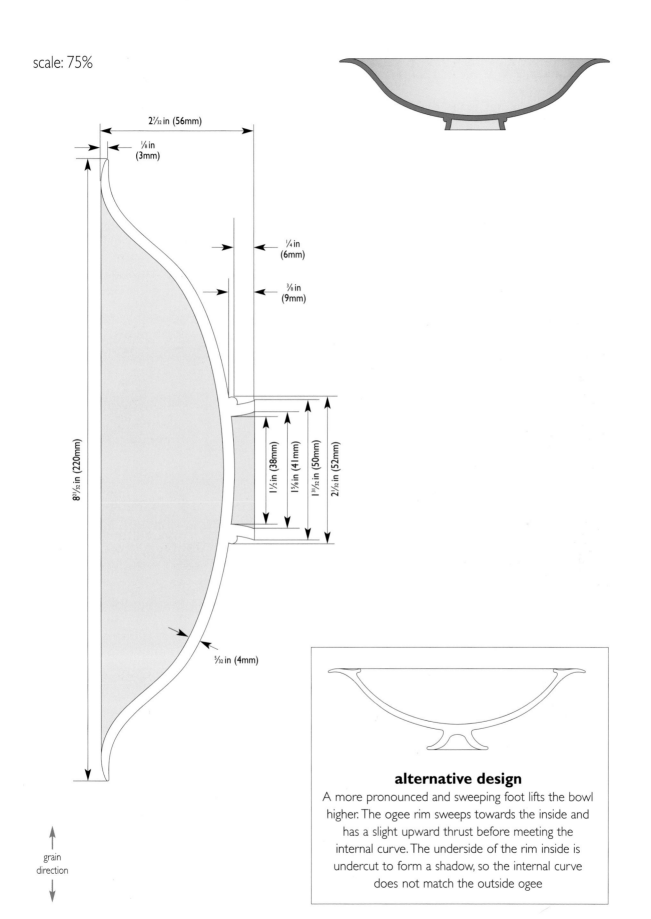

scale: 75%

2⁷⁄₃₂ in (56mm)

⅛ in
(3mm)

¼ in
(6mm)

⅜ in
(9mm)

8²¹⁄₃₂ in (220mm)

1½ in (38mm)

1⅝ in (41mm)

1¹³⁄₃₂ in (50mm)

2¹⁄₃₂ in (52mm)

⁵⁄₃₂ in (4mm)

grain
direction

alternative design

A more pronounced and sweeping foot lifts the bowl
higher. The ogee rim sweeps towards the inside and
has a slight upward thrust before meeting the
internal curve. The underside of the rim inside is
undercut to form a shadow, so the internal curve
does not match the outside ogee

4 bowl with rolled rim

box elder
Height: 1⅞in (48mm)
Diameter: 7¹³⁄₃₂in (188mm)

This bowl is a variation on the two previous designs, in that I have rolled over the top edge to create a drape effect. Do take time to play with shapes in this way – it is the only real way to learn what you like or dislike.

I chose box elder for this bowl for two reasons. One is that it cuts cleanly; the other is that it is not prone to fracturing, which makes it an ideal choice for this type of bowl, where the rim shape is potentially quite fragile. Box elder can be highly figured, as in this piece (although I have seen better figuring than this), but, as with most figured wood, you can never be sure what you will get until the end.

This bowl is dry-sanded, to avoid colour contamination, down to 400 grit, then oiled by hand with interior oil, and finished with a coat of wax.

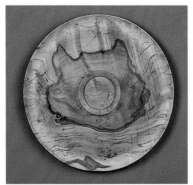

The internal profile of the foot is curved so as to lead the eye into the bottom inner section. Note the incised line to delineate the wall from the bottom curve. Be careful not to blur this area when sanding

hints
● **To refine the curve on the underside of the rim, the shear scraper is presented horizontally to the work in a conventional scraping mode**
● **Power-sanding makes light work of the finishing, but hand-sanding is necessary on the underside of the rim to make sure the profile is right**

tools used
⅜in (10mm) fingernail-profile bowl gouge
⅜in (10mm) square-ground bowl gouge
⅛in (3mm) parting tool
Tipped shear scraper
Abrasive down to 400 grit
Interior oil
Paste wax

scale: 75%

1⅞in (48mm)

⁷⁄₁₆in (11mm)

1¹¹⁄₁₆in (43mm)

⁹⁄₃₂in (7mm)

7¹³⁄₃₂in (188mm)

6½in (165mm) peak to peak

1½in (38mm)

1⅞in (48mm)

2in (51mm)

1½in (38mm)

³⁄₁₆in (5mm) constant

alternative design
A more radical roll-over of the rim gives the downward curve the appearance of drapes.
You could use scrap timber to experiment with the angle of this section

grain direction

5 bowl with incurved rim

burr elm
Height: 2½in (63mm)
Diameter: 9²⁷⁄₃₂in (250mm)

The bowls we have looked at so far have been open forms; this one has the rim enclosing the form somewhat. Again, this kind of shape is seen in many places and can be manipulated up, down, sideways and so on to create variations on a theme. Since there are no sharp edges on the curves, it handles well. Note that the widest part of the bowl is approximately two thirds up from the bottom. This is a pleasing ratio to the eye. Try experimenting and find out whether you agree or not.

The burr elm is a great timber to work, and to look at. The burr I had was tight and the grain did not pick out at all during the turning, leaving a smooth finish from the gouge that needed only a little tidying up with a shear scraper and abrasive.

This bowl is wet-sanded with oil as a lubricant, then power-buffed, with a final wipe-over with oil to finish it off. The whole bowl was power-sanded except for the foot, which was hand-sanded so as not to blur the details

Jumbo jaws do not hold well on the outside curve, so this piece is best gripped on the inside when detailing the foot. Take care: too much pressure may damage the rim, or even crack the side walls.

The shallow foot is undercut, and the underside sweeps up from the external wall of the foot to the shallow central dome

hints
● Always run a very fine piece of abrasive over the corners of the foot and rim to 'kill' the sharp edges
● Power sanding is a great time-saving method, but if you only have one arbor and keep on peeling off the abrasive discs to change the grades, the hook-and-loop-faced pads will delaminate or deteriorate quickly. Buy a couple of arbors and keep each of them for one grade of abrasive only, so it need not be changed until it is worn out. I know this means extra expense in the first place, but it will save both time and money in the long run

tools used
⅜in (10mm) fingernail-profile bowl gouge
⅜in (10mm) square-ground bowl gouge
⅛in (3mm) parting tool
Tipped shear scraper
Abrasive down to 400 grit
Danish oil
Power-buffing mop loaded with burnishing cream

scale: 60%

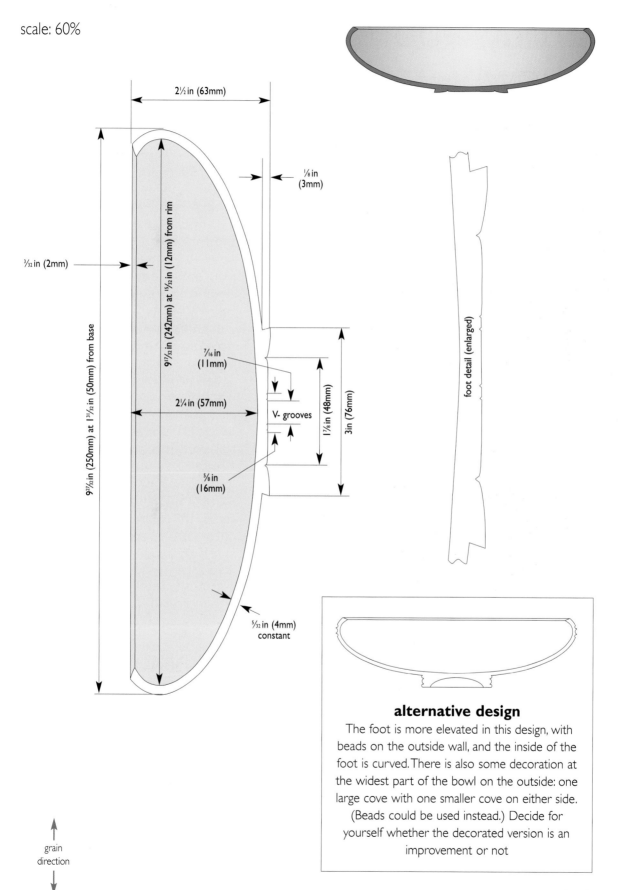

2½ in (63mm)

⅛ in (3mm)

³⁄₃₂ in (2mm)

9²⁷⁄₃₂ in (242mm) at ¹⁵⁄₃₂ in (12mm) from rim

9²⁷⁄₃₂ in (250mm) at 1³¹⁄₃₂ in (50mm) from base

7⁄₁₆ in (11mm)

2¼ in (57mm)

V- grooves

⅝ in (16mm)

1⅞ in (48mm)

3in (76mm)

⁵⁄₃₂ in (4mm) constant

foot detail (enlarged)

grain direction

alternative design
The foot is more elevated in this design, with beads on the outside wall, and the inside of the foot is curved. There is also some decoration at the widest part of the bowl on the outside: one large cove with one smaller cove on either side. (Beads could be used instead.) Decide for yourself whether the decorated version is an improvement or not

6 round-bottom bowl

cedar

Height: 3⅝in (92mm)
Diameter: 8²¹⁄₃₂in (210mm)

This bowl resembles the previous one but is a little higher, not as wide, and has no foot. The spigot on which it is held to turn the inside is completely removed afterwards. Once again it is gripped on the inside of the rim with jumbo jaws.

This piece of cedar has a wonderful golden colour to it, which would have looked fine on its own, but is enhanced by a knot section and stress figuring, resulting in ripples running across the work away from the knot.

A round-bottomed bowl is unstable when placed on a surface. If the wood is of a uniform density, the bowl will sit upright, but this piece is uneven since the knot is heavier than the rest, so it sits at a slight tilt. I do not mind this: the semi-enclosed form means that should this bowl be used to store anything, it will not fall out.

This piece was wet-sanded down to 600 grit using lemon oil as a lubricant, and finished with lemon oil for a matt surface.

A view of the underside, showing the smooth curvature and the figuring

hints

● If you do not like the round bottom sitting on the surface, make a ring from the same or contrasting timber and sit the bowl on that
● Using a slipstone to clean the flute of your gouge after grinding will improve the quality of the cutting edge no end

tools used

⅜in (10mm) fingernail-profile bowl gouge
⅜in (10mm) square-ground bowl gouge
⅛in (3mm) parting tool
Tipped shear scraper
Abrasive down to 600 grit
Lemon oil

scale: 60%

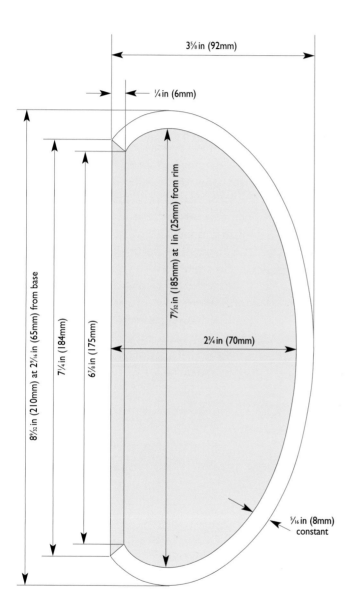

3⅝ in (92mm)

¼ in (6mm)

7⁹⁄₃₂ in (185mm) at 1in (25mm) from rim

8²⁹⁄₃₂ in (210mm) at 2⁹⁄₁₆ in (65mm) from base

7¼ in (184mm)

6⅞ in (175mm)

2¾ in (70mm)

⁵⁄₁₆ in (8mm) constant

grain
direction

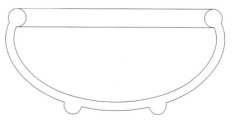

alternative design

This version has the same curved profile,
but the rim is in the shape of a bead,
made quite chunky in the manner of old
Roman pottery. The foot is formed by a
half-bead created from the spigot that
was used to hold the wood when
turning the inside

7 deep bowl

lime
Height: 3¹⁷⁄₃₂in (90mm)
Diameter: 4¹³⁄₃₂in (112mm)

Here is a taller semi-enclosed form. This piece can be held in a recess with serrated jaws. Again it is gripped on the inside of the rim with jumbo jaws to finish off the underneath. To make the foot, the recess on which it was held is merely cleaned up, the bottom domed slightly and a small flat created so that the bowl is stable when placed on a surface.

Again the widest part of the bowl is about two thirds of the way up, and there is some beaded decoration at this point on the external curve. This decoration is inset into the body so that the tops of the beads are at the same level as the outer curve of the bowl. The rim is coved, to add interest to this area and to lead the eye into the bowl.

The finished piece is wet-sanded down to 600 grit using lemon oil as a lubricant, and a further application of lemon oil gives a matt finish.

Here's how the rim and inside of the bowl look when viewed from the top

hints
● **Don't be tempted to skip grades of abrasives; this applies to hand-sanding as much as to power-sanding. If you start with 150grit, move on to 180, 240, 320 and 400 and so on until all scratches are removed. Remember to keep the abrasive moving across the surface at all times. If you stop, you will end up with annular scratches that are difficult to remove**
● **Reduce the lathe speed when sanding. This will enable the abrasives to cut, rather than glide over the surface burnishing but not cutting**

tools used
⅜in (10mm) fingernail-profile bowl
  gouge
⅜in (10mm) square-ground bowl
  gouge
⅛in (3mm) parting tool
³⁄₃₂in (2mm) fluted parting tool
Tipped shear scraper
Abrasive down to 600 grit
Lemon oil

scale: 100%

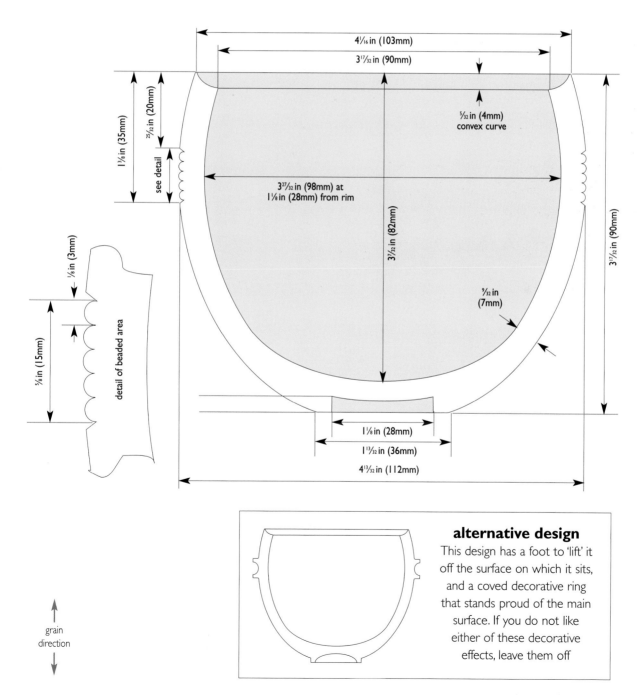

4¹/₁₆ in (103mm)

3¹⁷/₃₂ in (90mm)

⁵/₃₂ in (4mm)
convex curve

1⅛ in (35mm)

²⁵/₃₂ in (20mm)

see detail

3²⁷/₃₂ in (98mm) at
1⅛ in (28mm) from rim

3⁷/₃₂ in (82mm)

3¹⁷/₃₂ in (90mm)

⁹/₃₂ in
(7mm)

¹/₈ in (3mm)

⅝ in (15mm)

detail of beaded area

1⅛ in (28mm)

1¹³/₃₂ in (36mm)

4¹³/₃₂ in (112mm)

grain
direction

alternative design

This design has a foot to 'lift' it
off the surface on which it sits,
and a coved decorative ring
that stands proud of the main
surface. If you do not like
either of these decorative
effects, leave them off

8 flared bowl

quilted maple
Height: 1¹³⁄₁₆in (46mm)
Diameter: 7⅞in (200mm)

An open form, this bowl sweeps out from the base. The foot has two incised rings, seen clearly in the main picture, which correspond to the chucking points for the serrated jaws.

The swept foot and outer profile are created and finished first, then the bowl is reversed and located in the serrated jaws, which are gently tightened. It is important to note that although there is a slight hollow between the points where the jaws lock onto the foot, there must still be two points of contact for the serrations of the jaws to hold the bowl securely. Once the internal curve has been turned and finished, the bowl is held in jumbo jaws and the foot hollowed out so the underside of the foot mimics the internal curvature. The two incised rings are also added at this stage.

This piece of quilted maple has the quilting running through the centre of the blank, which gives a wonderful effect.

The piece is dry-sanded down to 600 grit and coated with a melamine lacquer finish thinned down 50%. This is then power-buffed with a mop loaded with burnishing cream, creating a satin finish.

The quilted effect is best seen from the top.
It looks like clouds or ripples in water

hints
● **Try to clean up the workshop the night before finishing is to start, so there is time for the dust to settle – especially when spraying or applying melamine finishes. Dust particles will stick to and mar a fresh surface coating**
● **Dovetail jaws are a suitable alternative to serrated jaws. It would just be a case of tidying up the bottom when reverse-chucked and then incising the decorative rings.**

tools used
⅜in (10mm) fingernail-profile bowl gouge
⅜in (10mm) square-ground bowl gouge
⅛in (3mm) parting tool
Tipped shear scraper
Abrasive down to 600 grit
Melamine lacquer, thinned 50%
Power-buffing mop loaded with burnishing cream

scale: 75%

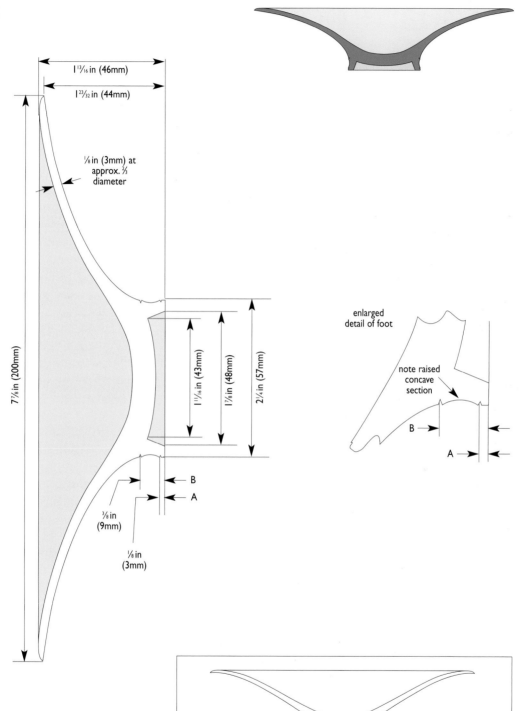

1¹³/₁₆ in (46mm)

1²³/₃₂ in (44mm)

⅛ in (3mm) at
approx. ⅔
diameter

7⅞ in (200mm)

1¹¹/₁₆ in (43mm)

1⅞ in (48mm)

2¼ in (57mm)

B

A

⅜ in
(9mm)

⅛ in
(3mm)

enlarged
detail of foot

note raised
concave
section

B →

A →

grain
direction

alternative design
Adding a pedestal foot to this bowl creates a totally
different look. This version is best held in dovetail jaws and
then reverse-chucked to finish the foot detail

9 square bowl

mountain laurel
Height: 1⁹⁄₁₆in (40mm)
Width: 6⅞in (175mm)

At some stage or other you will want to tackle a bowl or two that is not round. By using square-section blanks you are not wasting so much wood as when making round bowls. The trick is to have a perfectly square blank to start with; if not, the bowl will not be in the centre.

Mountain laurel is not prone to chipping, so I do not fit sacrificial strips around the edges. If you do fit these for added security – or because you are working with wood that chips – they are glued on at the beginning, then sanded or planed off once the turning is complete.

Turning the underneath is no problem, as the foot is held on the foot spigot and, as you are no doubt aware by now, the bowl will eventually be reversed-chucked in jumbo jaws while the foot is detailed. The hardest part of this project is creating a uniform thickness and keeping the square rim parallel. This is achieved by using the square-end scraper. Gentle cuts are made with a freshly honed cutting edge. Many light cuts will minimize flexing and reduce the need for sanding. Hand-sand the square sections with the lathe stationary. This will prevent rounding off the edges, or rapping your knuckles if you lose concentration.

The beads on the top (not shown in the drawing) are created with a ³⁄₃₂in (2mm) fluted parting tool, while the ones underneath are cut with a ⅜in (10mm) spindle gouge.

The piece is dry-sanded down to 600 grit and finished with a 50% thinned-down solution of melamine lacquer. This is power-buffed using a mop loaded with White Diamond to create a soft glow.

If you do chip the square rim, or find that it is slightly uneven, sand the edges on a belt sander until they are all nice and even, then finish them to the same standard as the rest of the bowl.

The underside shows clearly the beads at the intersection between the flat rim and the main body, and between the foot and main body curve

This shows the bowl from the top. The darker heartwood is clearly seen as distinct from the paler sapwood. The ripple figuring adds another dimension

tools used
⅜in (10mm) fingernail-profile bowl
    gouge
⅜in (10mm) square-ground bowl
    gouge
⅛in (3mm) parting tool
³⁄₃₂in (2mm) fluted parting tool
1in (25mm) square-end scraper
Tipped shear scraper
Abrasive down to 600 grit
Melamine lacquer
Power-buffing mop loaded with White
    Diamond finishing compound

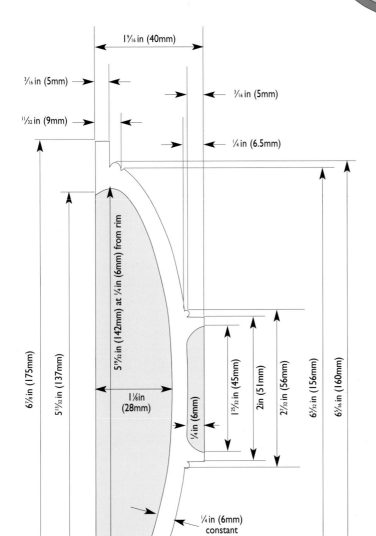

1¹⁵⁄₁₆ in (40mm)

³⁄₁₆ in (5mm)

³⁄₁₆ in (5mm)

¹¹⁄₃₂ in (9mm)

¼ in (6.5mm)

6⁷⁄₈ in (175mm)

5¹³⁄₃₂ in (137mm)

5¹⁹⁄₃₂ in (142mm) at ¼ in (6mm) from rim

1⅛ in (28mm)

¼ in (6mm)

1²⁵⁄₃₂ in (45mm)

2 in (51mm)

2⁷⁄₃₂ in (56mm)

6³⁄₃₂ in (156mm)

6⁵⁄₁₆ in (160mm)

¼ in (6mm)
constant

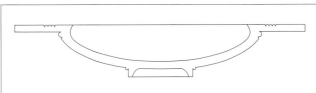

alternative design
The square rim can be extended further, as shown here.
Give it a go and see what you like

grain
direction

10 winged bowl

brown oak
Height: 1¹¹⁄₁₆in (43mm)
Width across corners: 13³⁄₁₆in (335mm)

This bowl is a cross between the previous piece and the rolled-rim bowl on pages 78–9. It sits on its wings so that the main bowl section is raised off the surface on which it rests.

The top has a flowing curve and the underside has the same curve running parallel to the top, but with a bead placed opposite the apex of the rim to add a bit of interest. This helps to define the underside of the round bowl section from the square wings. The bead is cut with a ⅜in (10mm) spindle gouge.

The underside at first has a spigot, by which the bowl is held while the top is turned. The bowl is then reversed and the spigot removed to create the smoothly curved underside.

This piece is dry-sanded down to 600 grit and finished with a 50% thinned-down solution of melamine lacquer. This is power-buffed using a mop loaded with White Diamond to give a soft sheen.

This underside view shows the bead which breaks the flow of the curve and sets off the main bowl part from the square wings

hints
● **Acrylic lacquer can be used instead of the melamine. Both give a durable finish; the acrylic lacquer just needs longer to cure before power-buffing**
● **If you do not have a belt sander to tidy up the square edge, glue a strip of abrasive with spray-mount onto your workbench, or onto a scrap of plywood or MDF (medium density fibreboard). Holding the work in your hands, rub it back and forth on the abrasive until the edges are even. You must remember to keep the bowl perpendicular**

tools used
⅜in (10mm) fingernail-profile bowl gouge
⅜in (10mm) square-ground bowl gouge
⅛in (3mm) parting tool
³⁄₃₂in (2mm) fluted parting tool
1in (25mm) square-end scraper
Tipped shear scraper
Abrasive down to 600 grit
Melamine lacquer
Power-buffing mop loaded with White Diamond finishing compound

scale: 50%

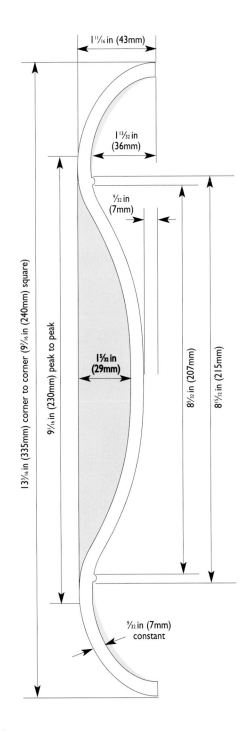

1¹¹⁄₁₆ in (43mm)

1¹³⁄₃₂ in
(36mm)

⁹⁄₃₂ in
(7mm)

1⁵⁄₃₂ in
(29mm)

8⁵⁄₃₂ in (207mm)

8¹⁵⁄₃₂ in (215mm)

13³⁄₁₆ in (335mm) corner to corner (9⁷⁄₁₆ in (240mm) square)

9ⁱ⁄₁₆ in (230mm) peak to peak

⁹⁄₃₂ in (7mm)
constant

grain
direction

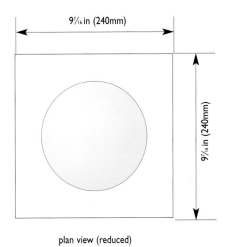

9⁷⁄₁₆ in (240mm)

9⁷⁄₁₆ in (240mm)

plan view (reduced)

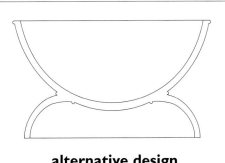

alternative design

The square wings extend from the main
body section in this design, giving a more
vessel-like appearance

platters

1 broad-
   rimmed
   platter

2 reversible
   platter

3 flat-rimmed
   platter

4 minimalist
   platter

5 simple
   curved
   platter

Platters are by definition shallow plates or dishes. A platter is to a turner like a canvas to a painter: the large diameter (compared to most bowls) allows you to concentrate on shapes which show off the figure of the wood and the quality of the turning to the fullest. Both functional and aesthetic, platters, by virtue of their sheer size, command a second look and make an attractive centrepiece for any table

    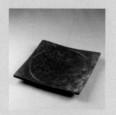

6 handled platter

7 roll-rimmed platter

8 platter with coved rim

9 sushi-style platter

10 square platter

broad-rimmed platter

yew
Height: 1½in (38mm)
Diameter: 16in (406mm)

A majestic centrepiece for a table or sideboard, this platter introduces all the skills you will need to complete the rest of the projects in this section.

The blank is first mounted on a screw chuck or faceplate, where the back is turned to completion. It is then reversed and mounted in a chuck which grips either on a spigot or in a recess. Once the top surface is finished, either reverse-chucking or hand detailing can be used to put the final touches to the foot section.

By now it should be clear to you that the techniques required for the various types of projects have a great deal in common. Repeated practice of these basic procedures is what enables us to develop, improving not only the speed with which we work, but also the dexterity and skill.

This platter is the only project in this book in which the use of a carving tool is suggested as an alternative way to create a finish on the foot.

Yew, as I have mentioned before, is one of my favourite timbers. The figuring and colouring that can occur within the wood keep me in a constant state of expectation when I am turning it. The only drawback is that the larger sections of yew that are available usually have bark inclusions or splits. I do not mind these, and think they even add to the attraction. See what you think.

Holes and fissures in the wood may be thought of as 'features' rather than blemishes

hints
- As before, a good size for the base is between ⅓ and ½ of the overall diameter
- The purpose of the foot is to raise the platter off the surface so that it appears to 'float'

tools used
½in (13mm) fingernail-profile bowl gouge with 45° bevel
½in (13mm) square-ground bowl gouge with 60° bevel
⅛in (3mm) parting tool
³⁄₃₂in (2mm) fluted parting tool
Tipped shear scraper
1in (25mm) square-end scraper
Deep-fluted carving gouge (optional)
Abrasive down to 600 grit
Sunflower oil
Power-buffing mop loaded with burnishing cream

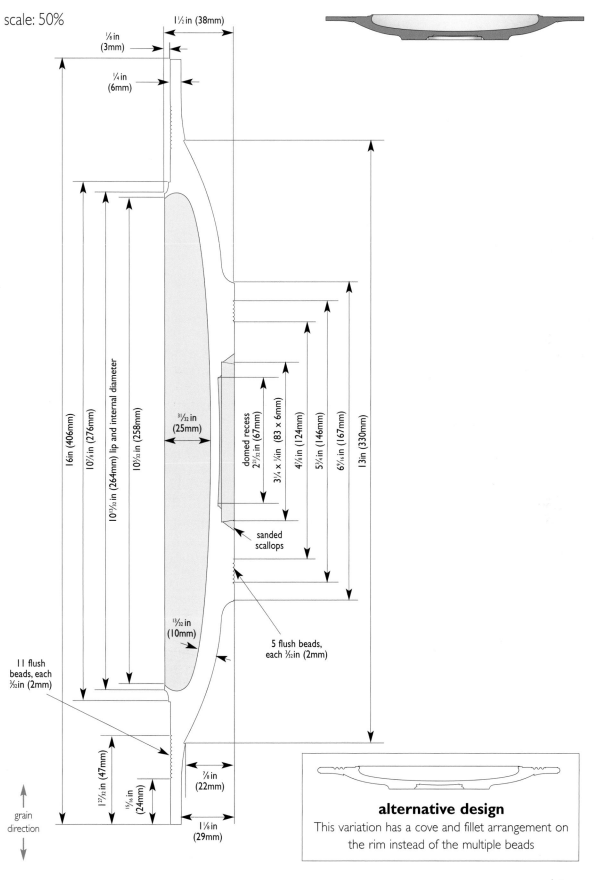

scale: 50%

1½in (38mm)

⅛in (3mm)

¼in (6mm)

16in (406mm)

10⅞in (276mm)

10¹³/₃₂in (264mm) lip and internal diameter

10⁵/₃₂in (258mm)

³¹/₃₂in (25mm)

domed recess 2²¹/₃₂in (67mm)

3¼ × ¼in (83 × 6mm)

4⅞in (124mm)

5¾in (146mm)

6⁹/₁₆in (167mm)

13in (330mm)

sanded scallops

¹³/₃₂in (10mm)

5 flush beads, each ³/₃₂in (2mm)

11 flush beads, each ³/₃₂in (2mm)

1²⁷/₃₂in (47mm)

¹⁵/₁₆in (24mm)

⅞in (22mm)

1⅛in (29mm)

grain direction

alternative design
This variation has a cove and fillet arrangement on the rim instead of the multiple beads

making the broad-rimmed platter

1 Find the centre of a piece of yew 16in (405mm) square by 1¾in (45mm) or so thick, drill a hole to suit your screw chuck and fix it to the blank. This chuck has screw holes in the flange for extra strength. When secure, mount it on the lathe. The side with the chuck will be the inside of the bowl. Position the rest about ¼in (6mm) below centre and far enough away not to foul the blank when it is revolved by hand

2 With the lathe set at about 500rpm, take a ½in (13mm) fingernail-profile gouge and make a pulling cut, with the bevel rubbing, from the centre towards the outer edge. Make a few passes to remove all the bumps. A ⅜in (10mm) gouge will work just as well – you'll just need to make a few more cuts

3 If the blank is very out of shape, as this one is, you will need to clean it up. If not, you can go straight to the next stage. Note that I am using a respirator that incorporates a face shield

7 Pass the scraper over the rest of the base, undercutting a little to ensure the base sits on its widest part without rocking. Now we are ready to profile the underside of the platter

8 With the same gouge as before, large, curved, sweeping pull cuts are made from the outer edge of the base toward the rim of the platter. Make sure you leave enough thickness to create the rim – a lot of wood may have to be removed to level the top face

12 One continuous pass across the surface of the wood will clean up the ripples. The profile of the underside is an ogee, with a quirk between the main body section and the rim. This is created at this stage with the gouge

13 A tipped shear scraper with the flat edge presented to the work at a 45° angle will clean up any small blemishes on the main body

14 The curved edge of the tipped scraper is used to clean up the underside of the rim

18 . . . and reapplying oil as necessary to keep the abrasive lubricated

19 Finish off by hand-sanding with 600 grit

4 Once the blank is true, speed up the lathe to about 1000 rpm and determine the diameter of the base

5 Cut a recess to the required depth and diameter to suit the size of the chuck jaws you are going to use. This one will have a dovetailed recess. Make a plunge cut to the required depth with the parting tool . . .

6 . . . then use the square-end scraper to remove the waste. A slight dome or button in the bottom of the recess adds interest, but leave a small flat at the edge of the recess to allow the jaws to seat properly

9 Dry yew does not produce long ribbons from this type of cut; instead, it produces chips of wood. This does not mean, though, that the surface is plucking out

10 Once you are nearing the required shape (which is a stylized ogee), make a delicate push cut to clean up the rim . . .

11 . . . and its outer edge

15 Now take the ³⁄₃₂in (2mm) fluted parting tool and apply some beads centrally between the recess and the outer edge of the base, to add some interest to this stark area

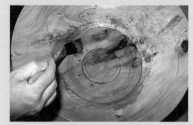

16 Brush on some oil – sunflower oil in this case, but your normal finishing oil will do, so long as it is food-safe –

17 – and power-sand to 400 grit, taking care not to round over the quirk near the rim . . .

20 Now power-buff using a mop loaded with burnishing cream

21 Once buffed, remove the blank from the screw chuck and mount it on the expanding jaws. Bring the rest parallel to the face of the bowl and set the speed to about 1000rpm

22 Take the square-ground bowl gouge and make a push cut from the outer rim towards the centre, stopping where the coved upstanding detail will be. Make as many cuts as necessary to remove the bumps and ripples

23 Use a freshly honed square-edge scraper to clean up the rim and make it flat

24 The freshly honed edge produces ribbons of shavings, even on yew. Now is also the time to create the boundaries of the upstanding coved detail, or fillet

25 There are some cracks in the rim area, as I expected, that need sealing or gluing to prevent them going any further

29 When you are nearing the fillet, change to the fingernail-profile gouge to create the undercut. Then shear-scrape the inner bowl of the platter, before using the fingernail-profile gouge to cut the cove on the fillet

30 Use the parting tool to define the outer edge of the fillet, then sand the rim down to 400 grit. Sanding now will prevent the beads from being damaged by sanding at a later stage

31 Now take the ⅒in (2mm) fluted parting tool and cut the beads into the rim section

33 Once the beads are cut, apply a liberal coat of oil over the work

34 Power-sand the internal bowl section down to 400 grit, then hand-sand the whole piece, including beads, to 600 grit, to remove any little blemishes

35 Power-buff the surface with the same mop and compound used for the underneath. The rim has already been sanded prior to cutting the beads, so it only needs buffing

37 Now take the platter off the jaws and place face down on a bench, with a piece of cloth underneath to prevent marking the platter

We can treat the wall of the recess in four different ways:
1 Take a carving gouge and carve some scallops around the edge to disguise the chuck dovetail (photo 37)
2 Power-sand some scallops, which is easier than carving them. Since my jumbo jaws are not big enough to hold this piece, this is the option I took (photo 38)
3 Gripping the platter in jumbo jaws (these would have to be large ones), or using friction drive between centres, turn a cove or other such detail
4 Leave it alone

38 If you choose power sanding with something like a Dremel, work your way around the edge until all the scallops have been cut

26 Thin cyanoacrylate adhesive (superglue) is ideal. Make sure it fills the cracks; treat every one you can see, and allow to dry fully. Do not use accelerator, as this will cause a white residue to form, which is difficult to remove

27 Take the square-ground bowl gouge, and with a push cut start creating the bowl section of the platter. Make small arcing cuts from the face down to the centre, gradually working your way back to the inside of the fillet

28 Note that the flute is always pointing in the direction of travel, and the cutting takes place on the lower wing of the gouge

32 For evenly spaced, touching beads, place one wing of the flute into the outer edge of the previous bead, and then cut. Take gentle cuts to minimize grain damage. Carry on until you have sufficient beads

36 The beads may clog up a little with the buffing compound. If they do, a wipe over with a bit of kitchen paper will clean them up

39 Sand to 400 grit, oil and buff to a fine finish

Three views of the finished platter

2 reversible platter

ripple silver birch
Height: 1¾in (32mm)
Diameter: 13¹⁵⁄₃₂in (342mm)

This unusual design can be turned over to become a cheese board or cutting board. This was a commission, for which a drawing was supplied, and I thought it would be worth including because the double-sided principle is something you could explore further with other designs.

The blank is initially mounted on a screw chuck on what will be the hollowed face. Whilst on the screw chuck, the edge details are turned, and then these and the face are sanded down to 400 grit and oiled with sunflower oil. I chose sunflower oil because this is totally food-safe.

The platter is then held in jumbo jaws to turn the hollow platter face. This is just a simple, shallow curve which is deep enough to remove the screw-chuck hole. The hollow is rather more than half the thickness of the finished piece. For detail, a small bead is set into the outer rim.

Silver birch is a good choice for this project. It is fairly dense, holds detail, is close-grained, and often has figuring that makes the platter side stand out. Suitable alternatives include any of the fruitwoods (although the size required may be a problem), sycamore, maple or beech.

The chopping board or cheese board side has no decoration, just a nice smooth, flat surface for cutting on

hints
● When working on large, shallow concave surfaces, use as big a scraper as you can. The large contact area will make light work of levelling the ripples
● If you find it difficult cutting beads with a gouge on edges like this, try a purpose-made bead-forming tool instead

tools used
⅜in (10mm) fingernail-profile bowl gouge
⅛in (3mm) parting tool
³⁄₃₂in (2mm) fluted parting tool
1in (25mm) square-end scraper
1½in (38mm) shallow-domed scraper
Abrasive down to 400 grit
Sunflower oil

scale: 40%

distances to opposite rim

13³²/₃₂ in (342mm)

13in (330mm)

12²⁹/₃₂ in (328mm)

12¹/₈ in (308mm)

11¹³/₁₆ in (301mm)

11²¹/₃₂ in (296mm)

1¼ in (32mm)

25/32 in (20mm) total internal depth

13in (330mm)

13¹⁵/₃₂ in (342mm)

13²⁵/₃₂ in (350mm)

³/₃₂ in (2.5mm)

³/₁₆ in (5mm)

rim detail (enlarged)

note inward slope

¹/₁₆ in (1.5mm)

³/₃₂ in (2mm)

⁵/₁₆ in (8mm)

⁵/₁₆ in (8mm)

⁷/₁₆ in (11mm)

⁷/₁₆ in (11mm)

1¼ in (32mm)

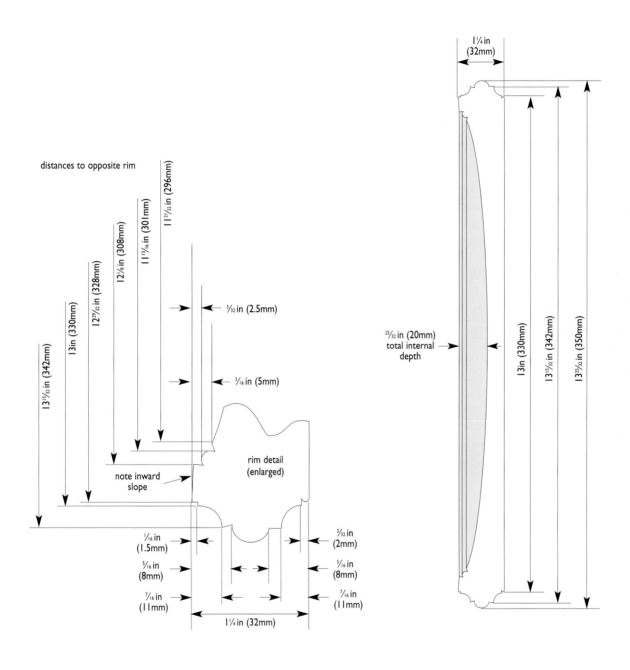

grain direction

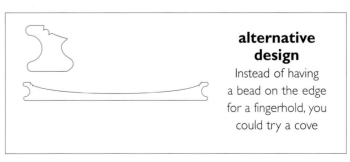

alternative design

Instead of having a bead on the edge for a fingerhold, you could try a cove

3 flat-rimmed platter

ambrosia maple

Height: 1¹³⁄₃₂in (36mm)
Diameter: 10⁷⁄₁₆in (265mm)

Here's a small, footed platter with a flat rim to pick it up by. The ambrosia maple is highly figured and the simple form sets off this figuring nicely. The undercut rim creates a nice shadow, and when the platter is turned over there is a little more detail in the added beads.

Serrated jaws are used to hold the platter in the recess of the foot. There is an incised line where the jaws gripped; this is created with the parting tool and is part of the design. Should the platter become damaged, it should be possible to mount it on the lathe again and refinish it.

The platter is held in jumbo jaws to finish off the underside.

It is wet-sanded down to 400 grit with sunflower oil as both lubricant and finish.

The shadow cast by the undercut rim adds interest, giving the impression that the bowl is deeper than it actually is. The rim provides a good fingerhold for lifting, and the foot raises the platter off the surface on which it sits.

The underside view shows foot and rim details

hints
● When using highly figured timbers, simple designs with clean lines are usually more effective. In this case, if you find the bead details clash with the figure, leave them off. These designs are meant as starting blocks, and can be adapted to suit your own requirements

tools used
⅜in (10mm) fingernail-profile bowl gouge
⅜in (10mm) square-ground bowl gouge
⅛in (3mm) parting tool
³⁄₃₂in (2mm) fluted parting tool
Tipped shear scraper
Abrasive down to 600 grit
Sunflower oil

scale: 60%

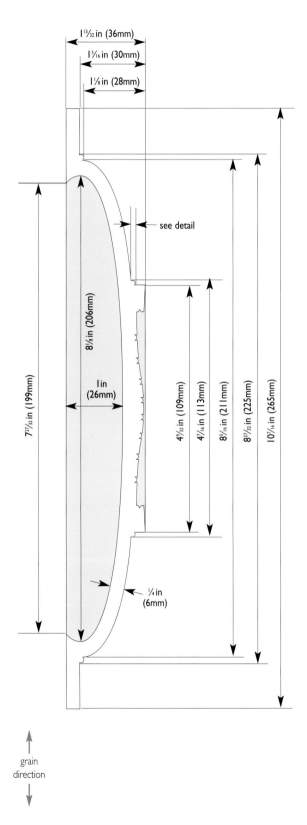

1¹³⁄₃₂ in (36mm)

1³⁄₁₆ in (30mm)

1⅛ in (28mm)

see detail

8⅛ in (206mm)

1 in (26mm)

7²⁷⁄₃₂ in (199mm)

4⁹⁄₃₂ in (109mm)

4⁷⁄₁₆ in (113mm)

8⁵⁄₁₆ in (211mm)

8²⁷⁄₃₂ in (225mm)

10⁷⁄₁₆ in (265mm)

¼ in (6mm)

grain direction

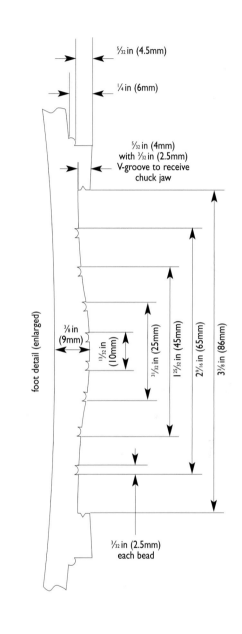

⁵⁄₃₂ in (4.5mm)

¼ in (6mm)

⁵⁄₃₂ in (4mm)
with ³⁄₃₂ in (2.5mm)
V-groove to receive
chuck jaw

foot detail (enlarged)

⅜ in (9mm)

¹³⁄₃₂ in (10mm)

³¹⁄₃₂ in (25mm)

1²⁵⁄₃₂ in (45mm)

2⁹⁄₁₆ in (65mm)

3⅜ in (86mm)

³⁄₃₂ in (2.5mm)
each bead

alternative design

This design has the rim set down a little from
the top, leaving an upstanding beaded fillet that
continues the curve of the underside

4 minimalist platter

European ash
Height: ⅞in (22mm)
Diameter: 12in (305mm)

This has to be one of the simplest platter designs around. It is a wide ogee profile, and the only decoration is a small recessed button in the base.

This platter is held on a screw chuck to turn the underside. A shallow dovetailed recess is cut underneath with which to mount it while the face is turned. Once the face is finished, the platter is held in jumbo jaws while the dovetailed recess is turned away and the decorative button created. The base on which the platter sits is just under half the overall diameter, which makes it particularly stable.

It is wet-sanded to 400 grit using sunflower oil as both lubricant and finish.

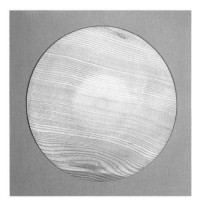

Ash has a pronounced grain structure which makes it well suited for this project. Far from being a boring, uniform colour, there are subtle variations across the platter. This picture clearly shows the subtle colour variations and strong grain definition, as well as the decorative recessed button on the underside

hints

● If you choose to power-sand your platters, use as large a sanding arbor as you can – 3, 4 or 5in (75, 100 or 125mm) if you can get them. These will make light work of the sanding process, nicely smoothing out any ripples

● It is best to use a slow speed when sanding, to allow the abrasive to cut; set the lathe to no more than about 500rpm. This also makes the abrasive last longer, and cuts down on the heat generated through friction

tools used

⅜in (10mm) fingernail-profile bowl gouge
⅜in (10mm) square-ground bowl gouge
⅛in (3mm) parting tool
³⁄₃₂in (2mm) fluted parting tool
Tipped shear scraper
Abrasive down to 400 grit
Sunflower oil

scale: 60%

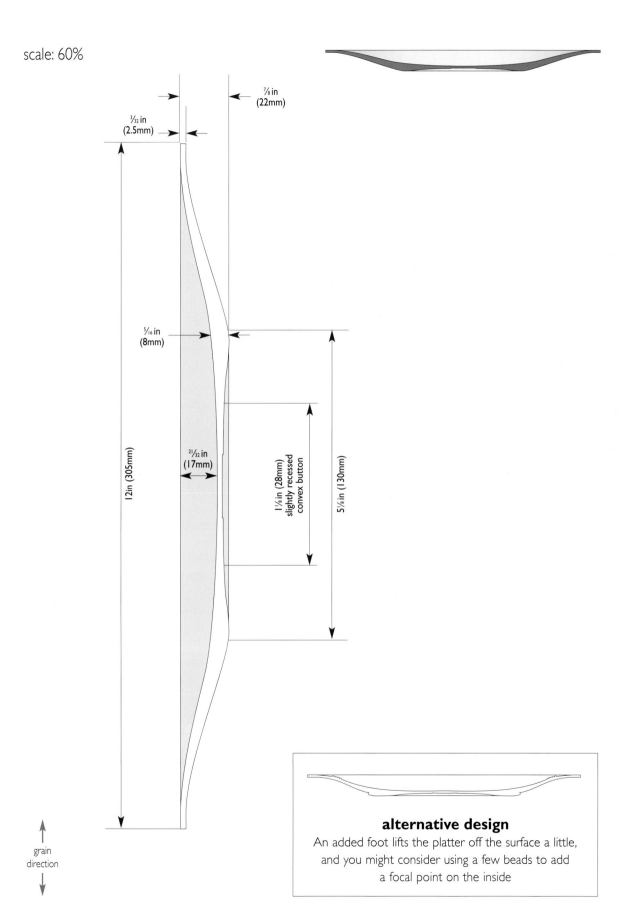

⁷⁄₈ in
(22mm)

³⁄₃₂ in
(2.5mm)

⁵⁄₁₆ in
(8mm)

²¹⁄₃₂ in
(17mm)

12in (305mm)

1¹⁄₈ in (28mm)
slightly recessed
convex button

5¹⁄₈ in (130mm)

grain
direction

alternative design
An added foot lifts the platter off the surface a little,
and you might consider using a few beads to add
a focal point on the inside

5 simple curved platter

mulberry
Height: 19/32in (15mm)
Diameter: 10 25/32in (274mm)

Mulberry is usually a rich yellow colour with a pleasant grain structure. I was surprised to see that this piece has a much darker, more defined grain that really stands out and almost shouts to be noticed. This is another simple design, and is turned in the same way as the previous one, but has a gentle upward sweep instead of the ogee profile. There is an upstanding fillet with a bead and cove sequence to add interest. Unbroken sweeps can sometimes look boring, and this is just one way of creating a break in the curve. What do you think?

The most difficult aspect of this one is the thickness. At 7/8in (22mm) the blank was very thin to start with, and at 1/4in (6mm) the wall thickness is a little less than I would normally use for a platter of this size, but the end result was well worth the effort.

The whole piece is dry-sanded to 400 grit and finished with sunflower oil.

Once again I have used beads to define the base and add interest to the underside

hints

● **On thin work, use freshly sharpened tools and take gentle cuts. Pushing the tool hard against the work will result in unnecessary flexing of the walls and could ruin the work**

● **Do not clamp the jumbo jaws too tight or you will deform the platter, wrecking any chances of achieving a fine finish on the underside**

tools used

3/8in (10mm) fingernail-profile bowl
    gouge
3/8in (10mm) square-ground bowl
    gouge
1/8in (3mm) parting tool
3/32in (2mm) fluted parting tool
Tipped shear scraper
Abrasive down to 400 grit
Sunflower oil

scale: 60%

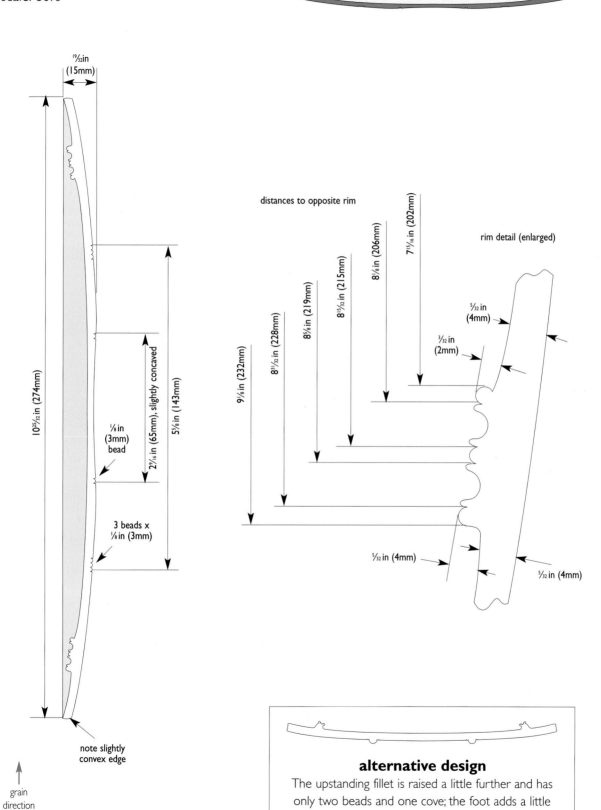

¹⁹⁄₃₂ in
(15mm)

10²⁵⁄₃₂ in (274mm)

⅛ in
(3mm)
bead

2⁹⁄₁₆ in (65mm), slightly concaved

5⅝ in (143mm)

3 beads x
⅛ in (3mm)

note slightly
convex edge

grain
direction

distances to opposite rim

9⅛ in (232mm)

8³¹⁄₃₂ in (228mm)

8⅝ in (219mm)

8¹⁵⁄₃₂ in (215mm)

8⅛ in (206mm)

7¹⁵⁄₁₆ in (202mm)

rim detail (enlarged)

⁵⁄₃₂ in
(4mm)

³⁄₃₂ in
(2mm)

⁵⁄₃₂ in (4mm)

⁵⁄₃₂ in (4mm)

alternative design
The upstanding fillet is raised a little further and has
only two beads and one cove; the foot adds a little
something

6 handled platter

European ripple maple
Height: 1⅚in (33mm)
Diameter: 12¼in (310mm)

A variant of the simple ogee form, this platter is provided with a continuous 'handle' with which to hold it. The undercut, recurved edge of the main bowl section meets with an inset coved fillet that is lower than the highest part of the rim. This coved fillet frames the opening and creates a nice focal point for the eye. Directly opposite the cove on the underside of the platter is a quirk, which visually separates the main body curve from the rim.

This piece of maple has a pink tinge to it which, combined with the ripples that run in two bands across the piece, gives a fascinating visual texture.

The platter is wet-sanded to 400 grit, with sunflower oil as finish and lubricant.

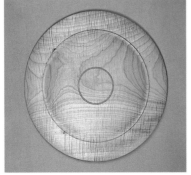

This view shows the simple curve on the base area, with a single bead to add interest, and the quirk which delineates the main body curve from the rim

hints
● Diamond files are great for honing, and create a good cutting edge on tools, but ceramic stones are, in my opinion, even better
● Remember to dispose of oily rags properly; they may combust and start a fire if you do not

tools used
⅜in (10mm) fingernail-profile bowl gouge
⅜in (10mm) square-ground bowl gouge
⅛in (3mm) parting tool
³⁄₃₂in (2mm) fluted parting tool
Tipped shear scraper
Abrasive down to 400 grit
Sunflower oil

scale: 50%

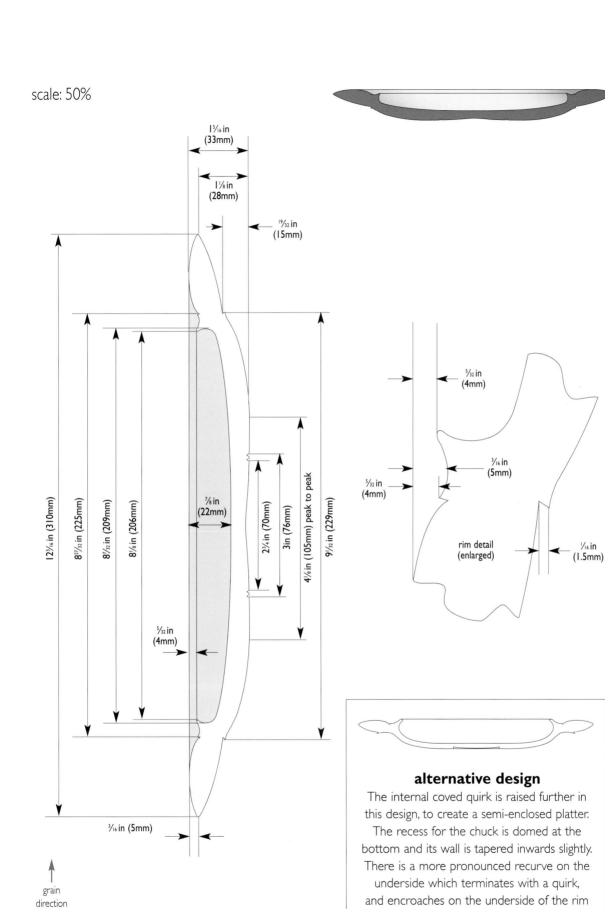

1 5/16 in (33mm)

1 1/8 in (28mm)

19/32 in (15mm)

12 3/16 in (310mm)

8 27/32 in (225mm)

8 7/32 in (209mm)

8 1/8 in (206mm)

7/8 in (22mm)

5/32 in (4mm)

2 3/4 in (70mm)

3 in (76mm)

4 1/8 in (105mm) peak to peak

9 1/32 in (229mm)

3/16 in (5mm)

grain
direction

5/32 in (4mm)

3/16 in (5mm)

5/32 in (4mm)

rim detail (enlarged)

1/16 in (1.5mm)

alternative design

The internal coved quirk is raised further in this design, to create a semi-enclosed platter. The recess for the chuck is domed at the bottom and its wall is tapered inwards slightly. There is a more pronounced recurve on the underside which terminates with a quirk, and encroaches on the underside of the rim rather more than in the main design

7 roll-rimmed platter

sweet chestnut
Height: 2⁷⁄₃₂in (56mm)
Diameter: 16⅝in (422mm)

This platter is similar to the previous one, but has a more pronounced domed rim that is undercut on its inner edge, the undercut in turn flowing into a gentle curve to the centre of the bowl. The rim on the underside has to be shortened to maintain enough wall thickness opposite the undercut. The underside of the rim is still domed, and provides a nice handhold with which to lift the platter.

One side of this piece is highly figured, the wood probably having come from a crotch section of the tree. The colouring and the flame-like figuring are shown off to the fullest with this large platter, as you can see especially in the top view below.

The platter is dry-sanded (to avoid colour contamination) to 400 grit. It is then finished with sunflower oil, and finally power-buffed using a mop loaded with burnishing cream.

The foot and the underside of the rim are clearly shown here. The button inside the foot was originally the bottom of the chuck recess

The figuring is clearly shown here. The simple domed rim does not distract the eye, but clearly defines the inner bowl from the rim

tools used

½in (13mm) fingernail-profile bowl gouge
½in (13mm) square-ground bowl gouge
⅛in (3mm) parting tool
1½in (38mm) shallow-domed scraper
Tipped shear scraper
Abrasive down to 400 grit
Sunflower oil
Power-buffing mop loaded with burnishing cream

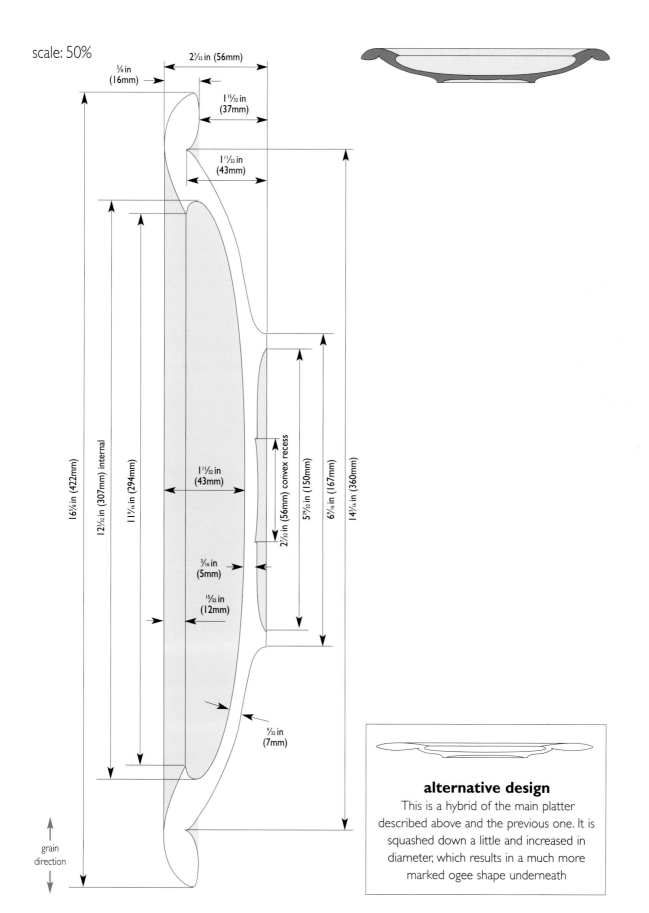

scale: 50%

2⁷/₃₂ in (56mm)

⁵/₈ in (16mm)

1¹⁵/₃₂ in (37mm)

1¹¹/₃₂ in (43mm)

1¹¹/₃₂ in (43mm)

2⁷/₃₂ in (56mm) convex recess

5²⁹/₃₂ in (150mm)

6⁹/₁₆ in (167mm)

14¹/₁₆ in (360mm)

³/₁₆ in (5mm)

¹⁵/₃₂ in (12mm)

16⁵/₈ in (422mm)

12³/₃₂ in (307mm) internal

11⁹/₁₆ in (294mm)

⁹/₃₂ in (7mm)

grain direction

alternative design
This is a hybrid of the main platter described above and the previous one. It is squashed down a little and increased in diameter, which results in a much more marked ogee shape underneath

8 platter with coved rim

European sycamore
Height: 1¹³⁄₁₆in (46mm)
Diameter: 17²⁹⁄₃₂in (455mm)

A coved rim design is the main feature of this platter. An upstanding fillet defines the boundaries of the inner bowl and the rim. This fillet, which is canted towards the inner section, has one central bead. The fillet is undercut to create a crisp shadow in the bowl section.

This platter is first gripped in a recess, then reverse-turned to clean it up. There is now a button at what was the bottom of the recess. You may have gathered by now that I like buttons on the undersides of my turnings.

The rim has a bead underneath where it meets the body, and there is another at the transition point between the body curve and the foot.

Sycamore is available in large sizes, which makes it ideal for platter work. It is also odourless and non-toxic, which is why it has traditionally been favoured for food use.

The platter is wet-sanded to 400 grit with sunflower oil as both lubricant and finish, then power-buffed using a mop loaded with burnishing cream.

The central button and the beads at the transition points all add definition to the underside

The upstanding fillet with its inset bead is clearly shown in this view, as is the subtle grain patterning

tools used
½in (13mm) fingernail-profile bowl gouge
½in (13mm) square-ground bowl gouge
⅛in (3mm) parting tool
1½in (38mm) shallow-domed scraper
Tipped shear scraper
Abrasive down to 400 grit
Sunflower oil
Power-buffing mop loaded with burnishing cream

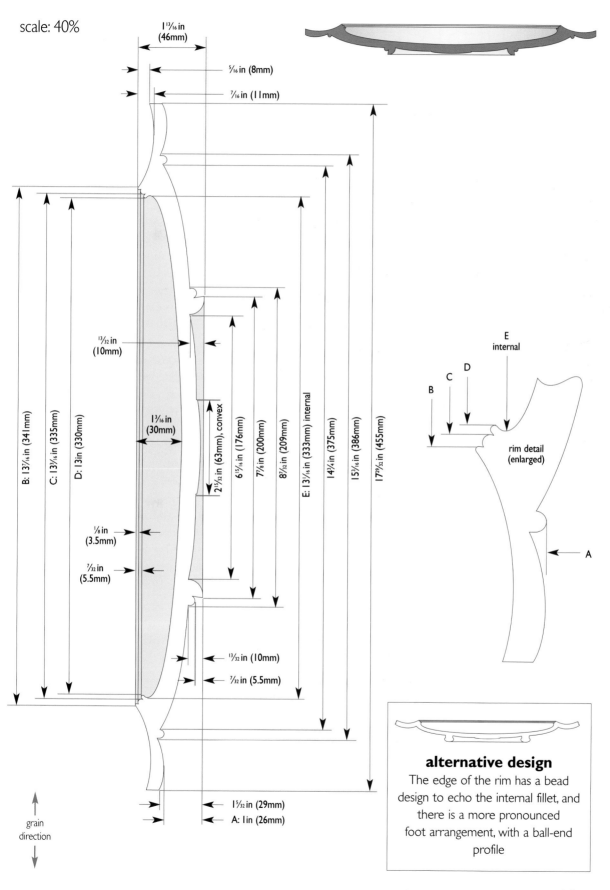

scale: 40%

1¹³⁄₁₆ in (46mm)

⁵⁄₁₆ in (8mm)

⁷⁄₁₆ in (11mm)

¹³⁄₃₂ in (10mm)

1³⁄₁₆ in (30mm)

⅛ in (3.5mm)

⁷⁄₃₂ in (5.5mm)

B: 13⁷⁄₁₆ in (341mm)

C: 13³⁄₁₆ in (335mm)

D: 13 in (330mm)

2¹⁵⁄₃₂ in (63mm), convex

6¹⁵⁄₁₆ in (176mm)

7⅞ in (200mm)

8⁷⁄₃₂ in (209mm)

E: 13³⁄₁₆ in (333mm) internal

14¾ in (375mm)

15³⁄₁₆ in (386mm)

17²⁹⁄₃₂ in (455mm)

¹³⁄₃₂ in (10mm)

⁷⁄₃₂ in (5.5mm)

1⁵⁄₃₂ in (29mm)

A: 1 in (26mm)

grain direction

B

C

D

E internal

rim detail (enlarged)

A

alternative design

The edge of the rim has a bead design to echo the internal fillet, and there is a more pronounced foot arrangement, with a ball-end profile

9 sushi-style platter

This square-edged platter with its simple curvature mimics the Japanese ceramic sushi dishes.

After initial mounting on a screw chuck, the underneath is turned, including the beads, and a spigot which has a central recessed dot made with a parting tool. The underside is sanded and finished. The spigot is then held in a chuck while the top is turned, sanded and finished.

ripple walnut
Height: 1⅜in (35mm)
Width across corners: 13⅞in (353mm)

The next stage is to reverse the piece and clean off the foot. The curvature of this platter prevents the jumbo jaws from locking onto the edge. Instead, a piece of plywood or MDF about 6in (150mm) in diameter, with a slightly domed face, is mounted on a screw chuck and padded with kitchen paper. The inside face of the platter is placed against the paper-covered ply, the tailstock assembly is brought up, and a revolving centre is located into the central dot in the spigot, ensuring full alignment. The revolving centre should be just tight enough to ensure that the platter is friction-driven without slipping. With the lathe set at about 300rpm, the spigot is then turned off, save for the central core held by the revolving centre; this is carved away once the platter is off the lathe, and sanded and finished to match the rest of the base. After this, the edges are cleaned up on a belt sander.

The whole piece is wet-sanded to 400 grit with sunflower oil as lubricant and finish, then power-buffed using a mop loaded with burnishing cream.

If necessary, the edges can be reinforced as described on page 88.

The flat base area is defined by a few 3⁄32in (2mm) beads. These could be replaced by V-cuts or left out altogether, if you prefer

The full figure of the walnut is shown on this top view. There is a bark inclusion on one edge; I like this, but if you do not, pick a clear piece of wood to start with

tools used
½in (13mm) fingernail-profile bowl gouge
½in (13mm) square-ground bowl gouge
⅛in (3mm) parting tool
3⁄32in (2mm) fluted parting tool
1½in (38mm) shallow-domed scraper
Tipped shear scraper
Abrasive down to 400 grit
Sunflower oil
Power-buffing mop loaded with burnishing cream

scale: 50%

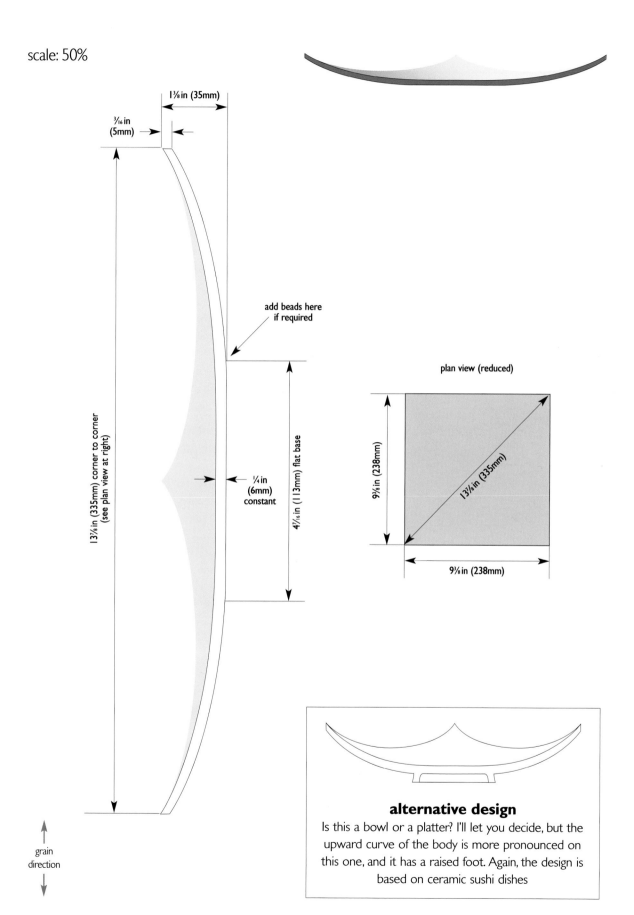

1³⁄₈ in (35mm)

³⁄₁₆ in (5mm)

13⅛ in (335mm) corner to corner (see plan view at right)

add beads here if required

4⁷⁄₁₆ in (113mm) flat base

¼ in (6mm) constant

grain direction

plan view (reduced)

9⅜ in (238mm)

13¼ in (335mm)

9⅜ in (238mm)

alternative design
Is this a bowl or a platter? I'll let you decide, but the upward curve of the body is more pronounced on this one, and it has a raised foot. Again, the design is based on ceramic sushi dishes

10 square platter

jarrah burr
Height: 1½in (38mm)
Width across corners: 16¾in (425mm)

This further adaptation of the sushi-bowl design is turned and mounted in the same way as the previous project. An inset bead design on the top serves to frame the main bowl and define it from the square wings. It comprises a ³⁄₃₂in (2mm) bead and a half-bead, set in so their tops are flush with the curvature.

The piece is dry-sanded to 400 grit with sunflower oil as the finish, then power-buffed using a mop loaded with burnishing cream.

tools used

½in (13mm) fingernail-profile bowl gouge
½in (13mm) square-ground bowl gouge
⅛in (3mm) parting tool
³⁄₃₂in (2mm) fluted parting tool
1½in (38mm) shallow-domed scraper
Tipped shear scraper
Abrasive down to 400 grit
Sunflower oil
Power-buffing mop loaded with burnishing cream

This picture of the underside shows the incised V and the quirk which set off the base and the square wings respectively. Those areas that show as lighter-coloured spots seem to have absorbed more oil than the rest. It is worth checking the finished piece after a little while, and recoating if you are unhappy with the appearance – as I should have done before this picture was taken!

The framed inner bowl is clearly visible here

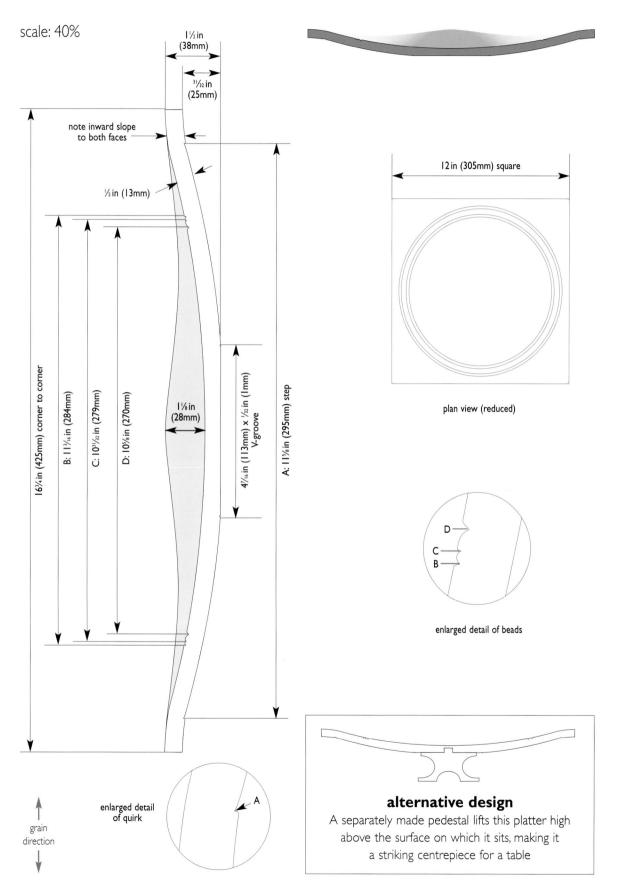

scale: 40%

1½ in (38mm)

3¹⁄₃₂ in (25mm)

note inward slope to both faces

½ in (13mm)

16¾ in (425mm) corner to corner

B: 11³⁄₁₆ in (284mm)

C: 10³¹⁄₃₂ in (279mm)

D: 10⁵⁄₈ in (270mm)

1¹⁄₈ in (28mm)

4⁷⁄₁₆ in (113mm) x ¹⁄₃₂ in (1mm) V-groove

A: 11⁵⁄₈ in (295mm) step

grain direction

enlarged detail of quirk

A

12 in (305mm) square

plan view (reduced)

D
C
B

enlarged detail of beads

alternative design

A separately made pedestal lifts this platter high above the surface on which it sits, making it a striking centrepiece for a table

hollow forms

1 oval form

2 egg-like form

3 spherical form

4 tapering form

5 upright oval form

Hollow forms always attract attention. The hollow within the piece is mysterious and redolent of things unknown. You only have to watch people at craft fairs to see the delight as they pick them up, turning them round to look at the shape from all angles, probing the depths of the hollow to see what's inside. As they handle each piece, they feel the weight to see how it matches their expectations.

Hollow forms can be created from logs or pre-cut blanks, and can have the grain running crosswise or lengthwise, to equally stunning effect. They do not have to be very large to create a dramatic impact. They look difficult to make, but with a little patience, working in a methodical manner and with a couple of specialist hollowing tools, you will succeed.

6 grecian form

7 teardrop form

8 mushroom form

9 form with scooped rim

10 pear form

oval form

she-oak
Height: 2²⁵⁄₃₂in (71mm)
Diameter: 8in (203mm)

This hollow form has a reasonably large opening and will provide a good starting point for exploring the techniques required for the projects that follow. The grain is running at 90° to the axial rotation of the lathe – in other words, the same direction as for platters and for all the bowls we have looked at so far. Some of the later projects will have the grain running parallel to the lathe axis, as in spindle work – as did most of the boxes described earlier.

You will find many similarities in the methods used throughout this section for holding and preparing the work; these techniques are common to nearly all turning projects. The following pages will expand your range by using all the skills learned on the boxes, bowls and platters, with the addition of working through small holes to create enclosed forms with straight, curved and undercut rims. This entails using some techniques and tools we have not encountered before, but they are not difficult to master as long as a few rules are observed.

She-oak was chosen for this project because it has a vivid orange colour and beautiful medullary ray figuring.

A view of the base, showing the beads

A top view showing the rim detail

tools used
½in (13mm) fingernail-profile bowl
    gouge with 45° bevel
½in (13mm) square-ground bowl
    gouge with 60° bevel
⅛in (3mm) parting tool
³⁄₃₂in (2mm) fluted parting tool
Tipped shear scraper
Hooked scraper
Hooked hollowing tool
Abrasive down to 600 grit
Danish oil

scale: 60%

detail of rim area (enlarged)

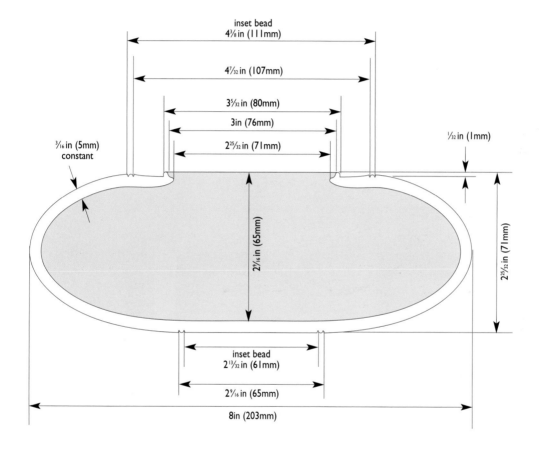

inset bead
4⅜ in (111mm)

4⁷⁄₃₂ in (107mm)

3⁵⁄₃₂ in (80mm)

3in (76mm)

2²⁵⁄₃₂ in (71mm)

³⁄₁₆ in (5mm)
constant

½ in (1mm)

2⁹⁄₁₆ in (65mm)

2²⁵⁄₃₂ in (71mm)

inset bead
2¹³⁄₃₂ in (61mm)

2⁹⁄₁₆ in (65mm)

8in (203mm)

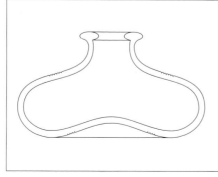

alternative design

This variant has an extended neck with a bead-like rim. It is also domed underneath like an old-fashioned bottle. An alternative to hollowing through the neck would be to do so through the bottom and reseal it later, as described on page 136

grain
direction

making the oval form

1 Find the centre of a blank of she-oak 3–3¼in (75–80mm) thick by 8¼in (210mm) wide. You can buy a centre-finder such as the one shown here …

2 … or make your own from a piece of Perspex or thick acrylic sheet. Score a series of concentric circles with dividers, then drill a central hole. It is then simply a case of finding which circle best matches the diameter of the blank, and marking through the hole

3 Drill a hole on this mark to suit your screw chuck, then mount the work on the lathe. The side with the chuck will become the top of the hollow form

7 True up the edge with a push cut. This will enable you to use a higher lathe speed for the following cuts

8 This hollow form will be held on a spigot, so speed up the lathe to about 1200 rpm and make a plunge cut with a parting tool at the required diameter and depth to suit the jaws you will be using

9 Take the bowl gouge and, with a push cut, undercut the bottom face of the spigot slightly to ensure that it seats properly in the chuck

13 Once all is clean and smooth, stop the lathe and remove the piece from the screw chuck. Now mount the spigot in the jaws of your chuck and secure it firmly

14 Adjust the rest to about ¼in (6mm) below centre and far enough away not to foul the wood when it is revolved by hand. Set the lathe to about 1200rpm and, using the bowl gouge, make a pull cut across the face to clean it up

15 Change to a push cut and make arcing cuts from the face towards the outer edge, gradually making bigger cuts as you work your way back to about 4in (100mm) from the centre

20 Because the opening in this piece is quite wide, you will find that a lot of wood can be removed with the gouge

21 The next stage is to measure the depth to which we need to hollow. This home-made device has a hole drilled through its wooden body to take a thin but strong rod of steel, about ³⁄₁₆in (5mm) thick. A second hole at right angles to the first holds a tapered wooden pin which locks the rod at the required depth

22 Take a hooked scraper, and adjust the rest if necessary so that you can hold the tool horizontal and cut on or just above the centre line. Hollowing, especially when learning, is best undertaken at slower speeds, so slow the lathe down to about 700rpm

4 Adjust the rest to about ¼in (6mm) below centre and far enough away not to foul the wood when it is revolved by hand

5 With the lathe set at about 800rpm, take a ½in (13mm) fingernail-profile gouge and, starting from the centre, make a pulling cut towards the outer edge, with the bevel rubbing throughout. Make a few passes to remove all the bumps. This will be the underside of the hollow form.

6 Once the face is true, change to a push cut and make arcing cuts from the face towards the outer edge, gradually working back to about 4in (100mm) from the centre. Aim for a nice even curve ending at half the blank thickness; the rest of the shape will be cut from the top face

10 Take the parting tool again and make a little dot in the centre of the spigot. This will be used to align it later on, when reversing it to turn off the spigot

11 Returning to the bowl gouge, use a pull cut down by the side of the spigot to remove the waste wood and refine the curved profile

12 Once complete, take a freshly honed tipped shear scraper and, offering the flat face at a 45° angle to the work, traverse it from the spigot towards the rim to clean up any small ripples and blemishes. Alternatively, use a square-ended scraper, presented in a conventional trailing cut

16 We are aiming for one smooth curve that mirrors the curve underneath and blends into it, leaving no sharp transitions

17 You may find that a final cut with a square-ground bowl gouge produces a finer finish

18 Make a plunge-cut with a parting tool at the diameter indicated in the main drawing to define the boundary of the opening

19 Use the fingernail bowl gouge to turn away as much of the interior as you can

23 Keeping the main, thick section of the blade flat and horizontal on the rest, feed the tip around the lip of the opening and take gentle cuts to remove the waste wood. The grain runs from the widest part of the hollow out towards the rim and down to the bottom; but, since these cuts are gentle, you can work the tool back and forth, leaving a little extral thickness so we can clean up the inside later

24 Shavings and chips will get thrown to the widest part of the cavity and will eventually prevent the tool from cutting. When this happens, stop the lathe, loosen the shavings with a finger or stick, and suck them out with a vacuum cleaner or extractor

25 An alternative to the hooked scraper is a cranked hollowing tool. This one has an articulated head section that enables the tip to be set at various angles. However, it is restricted in reach: the smaller the opening, the more of a crank is required to undercut the rim

26 Every so often, stop the lathe and check how far you have gone. You can check the wall thickness up to a point with your fingers, but at some stage a pair of callipers will be required

27 A hollowing tool with a larger crank or swan-neck is needed to undercut the rim fully. Note that the toolrest is set further away from the work for this tool: it is vital that the straight section of the tool is on the rest, and not the swan-neck or crank. The tip must remain in line with the central blade to ensure full control

28 Use this tool, or one of those mentioned earlier, to refine the interior. It is best to finish the underside of the rim area to final thickness first, then gradually work your way to the bottom. Check with callipers as you go

32 Use the same gouge to cut the wide, shallow concave feature that leads away from the opening, leaving an upstanding bead that frames the opening

33 Using the tipped shear scraper or a round-nosed scraper, clean up the concave detail, being careful not to destroy the bead

34 With a ½in (2mm) fluted parting tool, cut the bead that defines the outer boundary of the concave detail

35 The outer edge of the upstanding bead has a radius and an incised line that can be created with the fluted parting tool

39 While the outside is still wet, sand it using 600-grit abrasive, with the lathe running at about 600rpm

40 Once sanded, wipe over with a cloth coated in the oil

41 Now remove the hollow form from the lathe and remount using one of the methods described in the panel at right

43 Shear-scrape the surface, then sand to the same grade as the top

44 Cut the bead that defines the boundary of the base with a ½in (2mm) fluted parting tool

45 Oil and wet-sand the underside with 600-grit abrasive, remembering to wipe over with an oily cloth afterwards

29 The hooked scraper is used just to tidy up the bottom of the hollow. Remember to keep the blade flat on the rest at all times

30 To avoid the risk of getting your fingers trapped inside when sanding, use a purpose-made rod with an attached ball on which abrasive is mounted. Straight and cranked versions are available, or you can make your own from a stiff wooden or metal rod with some wadding on the end; abrasive is wrapped around this and held in place with adhesive tape. This is the only way to sand deep hollow forms. Some prefer to leave the tooled finish alone and not sand at all; the choice is yours. I sand down to 240 grit

31 After this, take the fingernail-profile gouge and cut the cove section on the inner rim, adjacent to the opening

36 Using fine abrasive, dry-sand the inner rim, quirk, cove and outer bead down to 400 grit

37 Then sand the outside of the hollow form. Power-sanding will be quicker than sanding by hand, but avoid the rim detail so as not to destroy or soften anything

38 The finish is Danish oil. With the lathe stopped, coat the outside down to the widest part, and all the inside. Applying it with a brush is quicker and more thorough than using a cloth

There are two ways to hold this piece while you turn away the spigot and finish the underside:

1 Line the chuck jaws with kitchen paper and expand them to grip on the inside of the rim. Bring up the tailstock for support, locating a revolving centre into the centre-mark we made earlier to ensure alignment. This is the method used in the photographs

2 Mount a scrap piece of wood in a chuck and turn a dome on the face; a piece about 6in (150mm) in diameter will do. Place the opening of the hollow form over the face of the dome, with a couple of layers of kitchen paper for padding. Use a revolving centre in the tailstock as before

Do not over-tighten the revolving centre; it should be just secure enough to ensure that the platter is friction-driven without slipping

42 Set the lathe at about 300rpm and turn away the spigot with a gouge; undercut the base slightly, leaving a central location plug for the drive centre

46 Once complete, remove the hollow form from the lathe and cut off the central spigot (I used a power-carving tool), then power-sand, oil and wet-sand to a fine finish

The completed oval form

2 egg-like form

burr yew
Height: 6¹⁷⁄₃₂in (166mm)
Diameter: 6²³⁄₃₂in (171mm)

This one is nice and easy, though care is needed to get the wall thickness right. The grain alignment is the same as for spindles, so the log is mounted initially between centres, with the pith off centre, and partially shaped using a spindle roughing gouge. (A fingernail-profile bowl gouge will also work well.) A chuck spigot is then turned on one end. Do not remove too much wood towards the spigot end, or it may flex during hollowing.

The blank is remounted in the chuck and the external profile refined from halfway down to the neck opening. Then, using the spindle gouge, take out as much of the internal timber as possible, as shown on pages 44–5. The gouge will only cut so far before it begins to flex; at this point change to the hollowing tool. Remember to have the rest at a height that allows the tool to be presented to the work horizontally, or trailing down a little, and cutting on or just above centre. Once the bulk of the waste has been removed, work down towards the base, finishing off a 1–2in (25–50mm) section at a time. This will minimize the distortion due to drying, and you should be able to achieve a uniform wall thickness.

Once the inside is done, finish-profile the outside down to the base, then sand and finish all over. Using friction drive between centres, remove the spigot and finish the base as described in the previous project. Wet-sand to 400 grit using lemon oil as lubricant and finish, then power-buff with EEE-Ultrashine.

The burr yew's pippy figuring is very attractive. A bark inclusion in the log has resulted in a void in the side wall.

The foot is less than ⅓ of the overall diameter, as in many hollow forms. The splits radiating from the pith of the log have been stabilized with cyanoacrylate. Some of them contain a white mineral deposit

hints
● Never grind tipped tools or 'shielded' cutters; hone them with a diamond or ceramic stone
● Instead of using oil as a sanding lubricant, you could try water. Allow it to dry off after the wet sanding, then rub over the whole thing with very fine abrasive before applying the finish

tools used
¾in (19mm) spindle roughing gouge
½in (13mm) fingernail-profile spindle gouge
Straight hollowing tool
⅜in (10mm) beading and parting tool
⅛in (3mm) parting tool
Abrasive down to 400 grit
Lemon oil
Power-buffing mop loaded with EEE-Ultrashine

scale: 60%

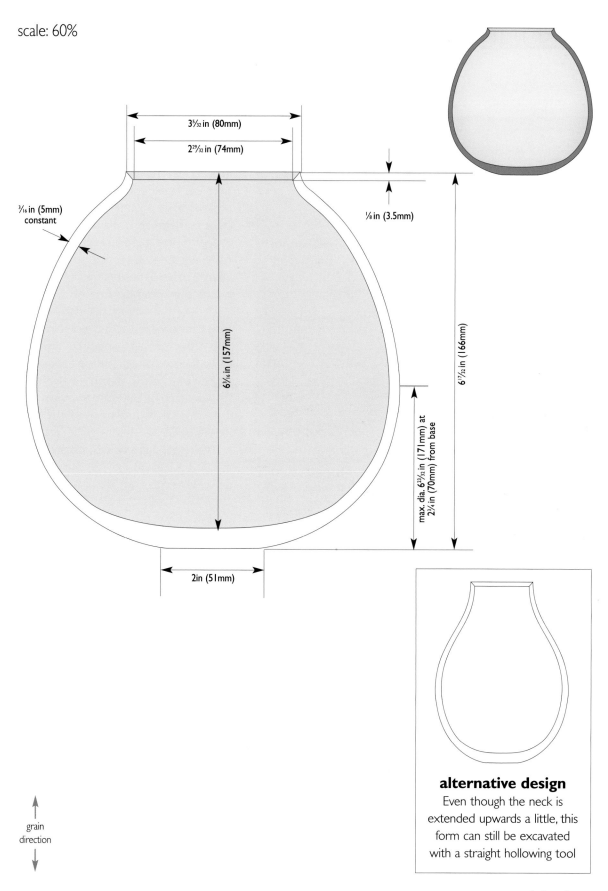

3⁵⁄₃₂ in (80mm)

2²⁹⁄₃₂ in (74mm)

³⁄₁₆ in (5mm)
constant

⅛ in (3.5mm)

6¹⁄₁₆ in (157mm)

6¹⁷⁄₃₂ in (166mm)

max. dia. 6²³⁄₃₂ in (171mm) at
2¾ in (70mm) from base

2in (51mm)

grain
direction

alternative design
Even though the neck is
extended upwards a little, this
form can still be excavated
with a straight hollowing tool

3 spherical form

damson
Height: 4½in (102mm)
Diameter: 5in (127mm)

Based on a ball, this is another hollow form that could be completed with a straight hollowing tool. Come to think of it, it's such a small project (although, like any piece in this book, it can be scaled up or down as you like) that the final finishing inside could be done with a round-nosed scraper. Turning and finishing are carried out in the same way as for the previous project. There is a beaded rim motif which 'frames' the opening.

Damson is a fantastic wood to work with. It is close-grained and cuts a treat. That is true of all fruitwoods, but damson, I have found, is one of the most consistent for beautiful figuring. The only drawback is that I have never been able to obtain it in large sizes. I think you will agree that it looks stunning.

The hollow form was dry-sanded down to 600 grit, finished with lemon oil and power-buffed to a fine finish.

The figuring shows even more clearly in the underside view

hints
● Instead of an oil finish, you could try an acrylic lacquer which can be power-buffed once fully cured. This will create a higher-gloss finish, which you may prefer
● There are many hollowing tools available at varying prices; a good one to start with is a tipped hollowing tool with a straight shank, that enables you to move the tip to different offset angles. These do not cost the earth, and will enable you to undertake a lot of work before you consider spending money on a bigger tool for larger work

tools used
¾in (19mm) spindle roughing gouge
½in (13mm) fingernail-profile spindle gouge
Straight hollowing tool with articulated tip
⅜in (10mm) beading and parting tool
⅛in (3mm) parting tool
Abrasive down to 600 grit
Lemon oil
Power-buffing mop loaded with EEE-Ultrashine

scale: 75%

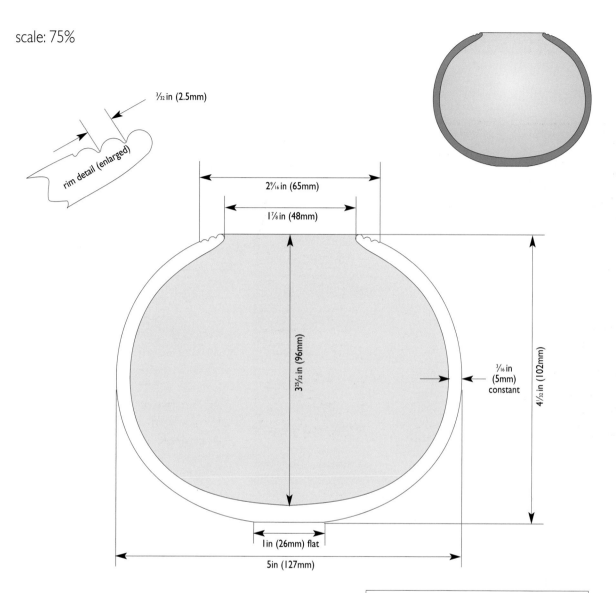

³⁄₃₂ in (2.5mm)

rim detail (enlarged)

2⁹⁄₁₆ in (65mm)

1⁷⁄₈ in (48mm)

3²³⁄₃₂ in (96mm)

³⁄₁₆ in (5mm) constant

4¹⁄₃₂ in (102mm)

1in (26mm) flat

5in (127mm)

grain direction

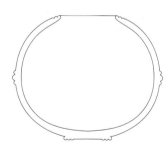

alternative design

This design has some bead decoration on the widest part of the curve, and a foot is added. I don't think I would use this beaded version on highly figured wood, but it can add interest to plainer-grained woods

4 tapering form

sumach
Height: 6¹¹⁄₁₆in (170mm)
Diameter: 4¹³⁄₃₂in (112mm)

When first turned, this piece was an almost iridescent green-brown. This picture was taken about 3–4 weeks after turning, and the colour has not diminished at all. I think you will agree, it's striking in its appearance. I have never found sumach in large sections, but the trunk sections available will enable you to turn some small hollow forms from it, like this one.

The shoulders are undercut here, so you will need a tool that will allow you to offset the tip a little to reach. The base is slightly undercut to enable the piece to sit securely on a surface without rocking, and it is turned in the same way as the first project in this section. The hole through which you work is still quite large; as your skills progress, you can reduce the size of the hole.

The hollow form is dry-sanded down to 600 grit, finished with lemon oil and power-buffed to a fine surface finish.

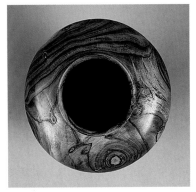

The grain looks totally different when viewed from another perspective

hints
● A simple way of gauging the depth of hollowing is to wrap a piece of coloured tape around the shank of the hollowing tool to indicate the maximum depth you must go to
● Remember: the further the hollowing tool overhangs the toolrest, the longer the handle needs to be to enable you to counter the downward forces exerted on the cutting edge

tools used
¾in (19mm) spindle roughing gouge
½in (13mm) fingernail-profile spindle gouge
Straight hollowing tool with articulated tip
⅜in (10mm) beading and parting tool
⅛in (3mm) parting tool
Abrasive down to 400 grit
Lemon oil
Power-buffing mop loaded with EEE-Ultrashine

scale: 75%

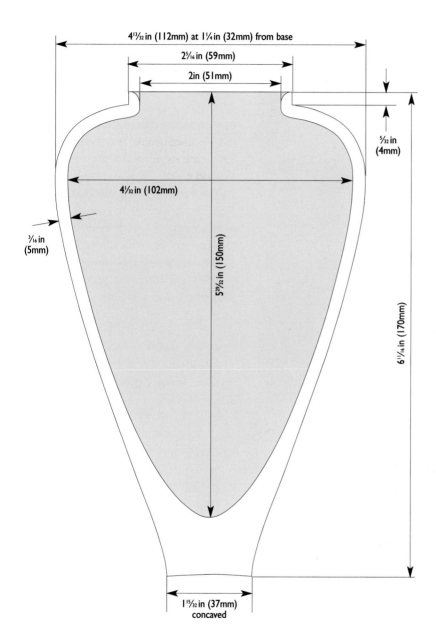

4¹³⁄₃₂ in (112mm) at 1¼ in (32mm) from base

2⁵⁄₁₆ in (59mm)

2in (51mm)

⁵⁄₃₂ in (4mm)

4¹⁄₃₂ in (102mm)

³⁄₁₆ in (5mm)

5²⁹⁄₃₂ in (150mm)

6¹¹⁄₁₆ in (170mm)

1¹⁵⁄₃₂ in (37mm)
concaved

grain direction

alternative design

By adding a flared-out rim and a foot which is detailed underneath, the look is altered radically, yet this is still only a small step away from the original design

5 upright oval form

pear
Height: 6½in (165mm)
Diameter: 3½in (89mm)

Pear is another wood that cuts well, but is not known for its wild or spectacular figuring. Instead it is more common to find a subtle, mottled appearance. This simple upright form is often seen in glass, and transfers readily to wood. Turned from a log, the underside has a distinct dimple, and the main body has a bark inclusion. The log was not fully dry, and it was vital to work inside the hollow from the rim down, finishing 1–2in (25–50mm) sections to completion as I went, in order to get an even wall thickness before distortion occurred.

The hollow form is dry-sanded down to 600 grit, finished with lemon oil and power-buffed to a fine finish.

tools used
¾in (19mm) spindle roughing gouge
½in (13mm) fingernail-profile spindle gouge
Straight hollowing tool with articulated tip
⅜in (10mm) beading and parting tool
⅛in (3mm) parting tool
³⁄₃₂in (2mm) fluted parting tool
Abrasive down to 400 grit
Lemon oil
Power-buffing mop loaded with EEE-Ultrashine

From the top, you can see clearly how simply the bead and cove design frames the opening

hints
● A simple form like this could be further decorated with beads around the body, much like the boxwood box on pages 58–9
● The dimple on the underside is not replicated inside. Instead, the interior has an even, rounded curve at the bottom. This leaves a thicker section in the base that gives additional weight and helps to make the item stable. This is a useful technique to remember for other hollow forms

scale: 75%

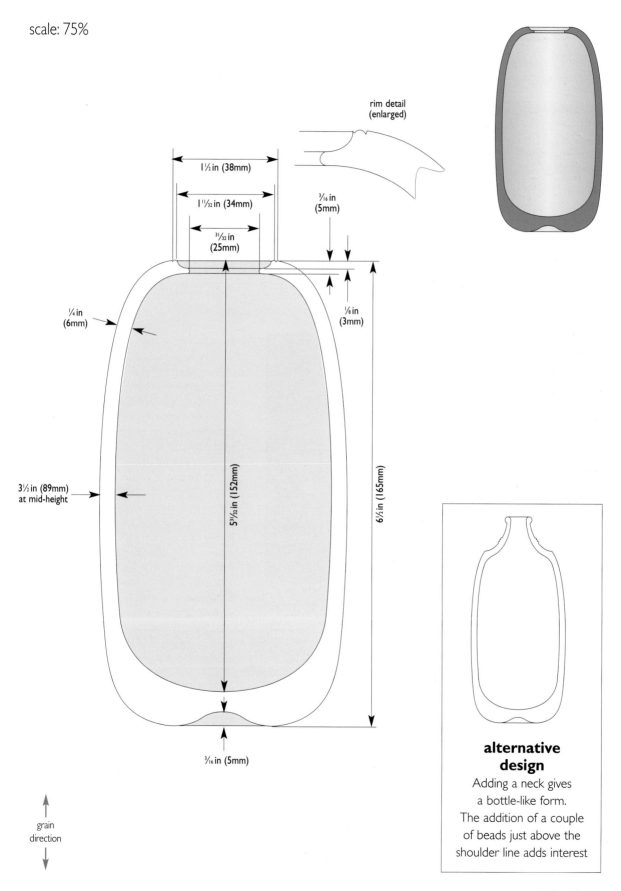

rim detail
(enlarged)

1½ in (38mm)

1¹¹⁄₃₂ in (34mm)

³⁄₁₆ in
(5mm)

³¹⁄₃₂ in
(25mm)

¼ in
(6mm)

⅛ in
(3mm)

5³¹⁄₃₂ in (152mm)

6½ in (165mm)

3½ in (89mm)
at mid-height

³⁄₁₆ in (5mm)

grain
direction

alternative
design

Adding a neck gives
a bottle-like form.
The addition of a couple
of beads just above the
shoulder line adds interest

6 grecian form

masur birch
Height: 7⁹⁄₃₂in (185mm)
Diameter: 6³⁄₈in (162mm)

The flecked markings characteristic of masur birch are well suited to this classical form. There are two ways to tackle this project. One is to follow the procedure described on pages 122–5, working through the narrow opening. The other is to turn the neck and body from the same piece of wood, separate them, and then rejoin them at a later stage. The choice is yours. Since I have already explained the first technique, I will now describe the second approach.

The underside view shows that the pith is just off centre

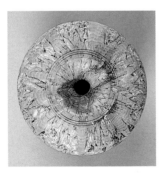

This view from the top shows the beads disguising the join

tools used

¾in (19mm) spindle roughing gouge
½in (13mm) fingernail-profile spindle gouge
Straight hollowing tool with articulated tip
Swan neck hollowing tool
⅜in (10mm) beading and parting tool
⅛in (3mm) parting tool
³⁄₃₂in (2mm) fluted parting tool
Abrasive down to 600 grit
Hard Burnishing Oil
Power-buffing mop loaded with EEE-Ultrashine

1 Mount the wood between centres, rough it down to a cylinder and then partly profile it with the roughing gouge. For the time being, leave the neck area at the headstock end as a parallel cylinder, just over the maximum diameter of the tapered opening in which it will be located.
2 Cut a spigot on the main body end to fit into the jaws of your chuck. Once cut, remove the work from the lathe and mount it in the chuck.
3 Cut a spigot on the neck end to suit your chuck, then use a ³⁄₃₂in (2mm) parting tool to part off the cylinder of wood that will be the neck, making the cut at the end nearest the body, to minimize grain misalignment.
4 Create a gentle taper or step in the opening, as shown in the drawing, then hollow out the cavity and finish the inside.
5 Remove the main body from the chuck and fit the neck into the chuck by means of its spigot. Turn a taper or step on the end to match the one cut on the main body, and check that it is a good secure fit. The grain should align reasonably well, although it will be a little off.
6 Once the join is cut, take a spindle gouge and bore a hole down the centre of the cylinder. Open it up to the required diameter and sweep back towards the outer join.
7 After cutting, sand the piece and remove it from the chuck. Remount the body, align the grain and Superglue the neck cylinder to the body, bringing the tailstock up for support.
8 Once set, blend in the main body curve with the neck, turn the cove, the rim and the opening at the top. Cut some beads with a ³⁄₃₂in (2mm) fluted parting tool around the join. The edge of one bead must be on the join; then place another alongside it. This will disguise the join and any grain misalignment.
9 Stop the lathe and feel inside to see if there is a ridge at the join. If there is, feed in a swan-neck hollowing tool and remove it.
10 Now remove the hollow form from the chuck and friction-drive it between centres to remove the spigot and create the base. Don't use too much pressure, or you may break the neck join.
11 The hollow form is dry-sanded down to 600 grit, finished with Hard Burnishing Oil and power-buffed to a fine finish.

scale: 60%

enlarged detail of joint

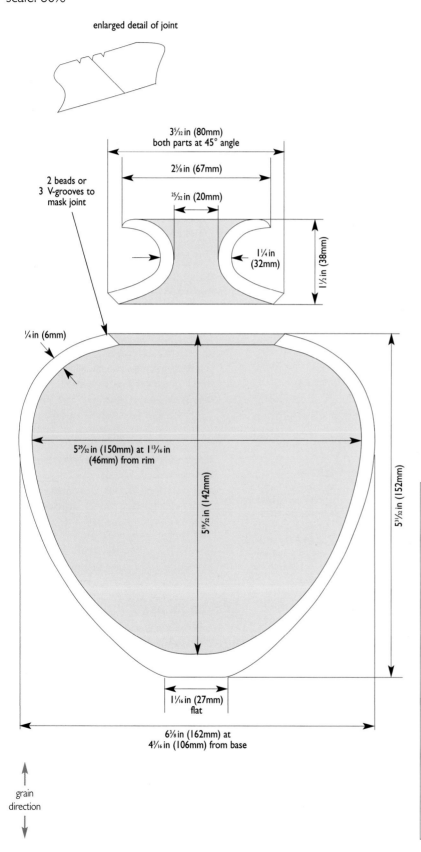

3⁵⁄₃₂ in (80mm)
both parts at 45° angle

2⁵⁄₈ in (67mm)

²⁵⁄₃₂ in (20mm)

2 beads or
3 V-grooves to
mask joint

1¼ in
(32mm)

1½ in (38mm)

¼ in (6mm)

5²⁹⁄₃₂ in (150mm) at 1¹³⁄₁₆ in
(46mm) from rim

5¹⁹⁄₃₂ in (142mm)

5³¹⁄₃₂ in (152mm)

1¹⁄₁₆ in (27mm)
flat

6³⁄₈ in (162mm) at
4³⁄₁₆ in (106mm) from base

grain
direction

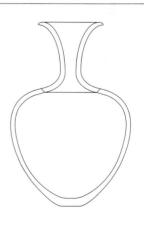

alternative
design

A longer neck gives a
bottle-like form similar in
style to those found in
classical Greek and Roman
pottery

7 teardrop form

spalted beech
Height: 4²⁹⁄₃₂in (125mm)
Diameter: 4¹¹⁄₃₂in (110mm)

Some forms do not allow easy access for hollowing out, and this is one such shape. Hollowing through the long neck would be almost impossible. One alternative is to cut the external profile only and leave it as a simple bud vase – otherwise known to turners as a 'weed pot'. Instead of a hollow inside, there would just be a ¼in (6mm) drill hole through the neck to allow a few stems of dried flowers to be placed in it.

I did hollow this one, but not through the neck. Instead, I hollowed through the bottom and then plugged the hole. The technique is similar to the one described previously, but there are a few differences.

Spalted patterning in beech can be very dramatic. Because there is no predicting where the fungal spores will go once in the wood, each piece will have a different pattern.

The underside, showing the bead which disguises the join

1 Rough the wood down between centres and partly profile it with the roughing gouge, leaving the neck area at the tailstock end as a parallel cylinder at least 2in (50mm) in diameter.
2 Cut a spigot on the neck end to fit your chuck, then form a parallel cylinder about 2in (50mm) diameter by ¾in (19mm) long on the other end. Remount the work in the chuck.
3 Cut a spigot to suit your chuck on the cylinder at the base end, then part off this section at the end nearest the body.
4 Create a gentle taper or step in what will be the opening, then hollow out the cavity and finish the inside to a point at the neck end. Do not bore the hole down the neck at this stage. Remove the main body from the chuck.
5 The cylinder that will be the base plug is now fitted to the chuck by means of its spigot. Create a taper to match the one cut on the main body, and check that it is a good secure fit.
6 Align the grain and glue the cylinder to the body, bringing up the tailstock for support.
7 Once set, remove the tailstock and bore the central hole in the neck. Clean up the rim before bringing up the tailstock again.
8 Profile the body and neck.
9 Sand and finish, then friction-drive the piece between centres to remove the spigot and detail the join in the foot with a small bead.
10 Dry-sand down to 600 grit, finish with Hard Burnishing Oil and power-buff to a fine finish.

hints
● **Use PVA instead of cyanoacrylate adhesive to bond the wood together. The PVA forms a stronger bond and excess glue can be wiped off immediately to prevent staining**
● **Spalted wood can be a bit spongy and may pick out. If this happens, soak the wood with a 50% thinned solution of melamine sanding sealer and let it dry. This will stabilize the wood and enable you to get a better cut**

tools used
¾in (19mm) spindle roughing gouge
½in (13mm) fingernail-profile spindle gouge
Straight hollowing tool with articulated tip
⅜in (10mm) beading and parting tool
⅛in (3mm) parting tool
³⁄₃₂in (2mm) fluted parting tool
Abrasive down to 600 grit
Hard Burnishing Oil
Power-buffing mop loaded with EEE-Ultrashine

scale: 100%

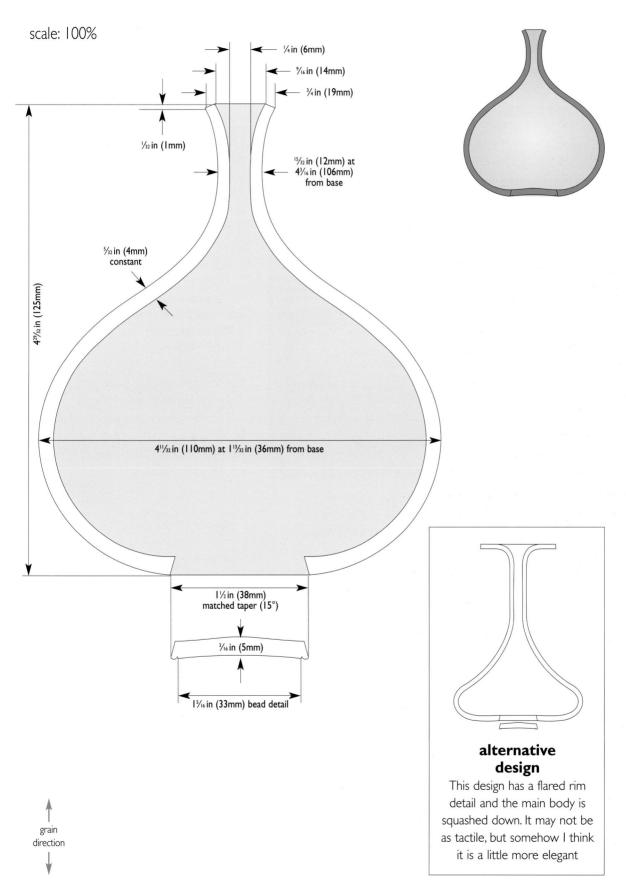

¼ in (6mm)

⁹⁄₁₆ in (14mm)

¾ in (19mm)

¹⁄₃₂ in (1mm)

¹⁵⁄₃₂ in (12mm) at
4³⁄₁₆ in (106mm)
from base

⁵⁄₃₂ in (4mm)
constant

4²⁹⁄₃₂ in (125mm)

4¹¹⁄₃₂ in (110mm) at 1¹³⁄₃₂ in (36mm) from base

1½ in (38mm)
matched taper (15°)

³⁄₁₆ in (5mm)

1⁵⁄₁₆ in (33mm) bead detail

grain
direction

alternative
design

This design has a flared rim
detail and the main body is
squashed down. It may not be
as tactile, but somehow I think
it is a little more elegant

8 mushroom form

ripple ash
Height: 1²¹⁄₃₂in (42mm)
Diameter: 5in (127mm)

This is a nice form to work on; it is a very tactile shape and begs to be picked up. The grain runs crosswise as with the first project in this section, and the techniques for turning it are the same, except that on this project the foot is not removed at the end, but simply refined to clean it up.

There is a large opening through which to work, which makes hollowing this piece nice and easy. The opening is framed by an inset cove detail, and the raised edge of this lies at the same level as the top of the domed shoulders.

The rippled ash used for this project not only cuts well, but adds a dramatic impact to the overall appearance.

The finished hollow form is wet-sanded to 600 grit with lemon oil as both lubricant and finish, then power-buffed to a fine finish.

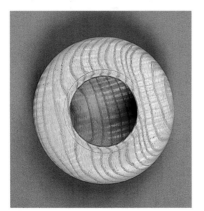

This view shows how the ripples run in two distinct bands across the wood. But note how they also extend well into the bottom of the cavity, to create another great effect

hints
● With a tipped hollowing tool it is best to have two cutters. The one with the smaller tip will hollow out quickly. The other needs to have a larger curvature to make the final finishing cuts
● If you plan to use hollow forms to store pot-pourri, coat the inside with a melamine finish to prevent the oil from the pot-pourri soaking through the wood and marring the surface on which the piece sits

tools used
⅜in (10mm) fingernail-profile gouge
Straight hollowing tool with
    articulated tip
⅜in (10mm) beading and parting tool
⅛in (3mm) parting tool
Abrasive down to 400 grit
Lemon oil
Power-buffing mop loaded with EEE-
    Ultrashine

scale: 100%

rim detail (enlarged)

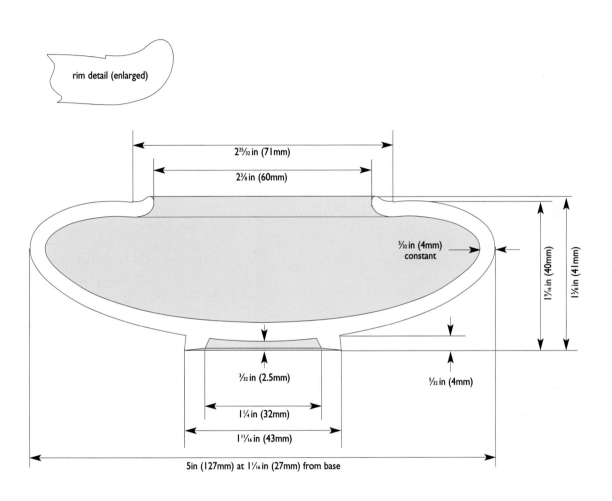

$2^{25}/_{32}$ in (71mm)

$2^{3}/_{8}$ in (60mm)

$^{5}/_{32}$ in (4mm)
constant

$1^{9}/_{16}$ in (40mm)

$1^{5}/_{8}$ in (41mm)

$^{3}/_{32}$ in (2.5mm)

$^{5}/_{32}$ in (4mm)

$1^{1}/_{4}$ in (32mm)

$1^{11}/_{16}$ in (43mm)

5in (127mm) at $1^{1}/_{16}$ in (27mm) from base

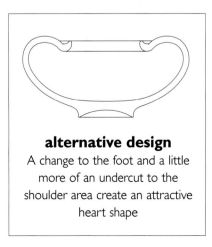

alternative design
A change to the foot and a little
more of an undercut to the
shoulder area create an attractive
heart shape

grain
direction

9 form with scooped rim

redwood burr
Height: 3⅝in (92mm)
Diameter: 5⁹⁄₃₂in (134mm)

This is a taller version of the form we have just worked on. The grain is running from top to bottom on this project, so the techniques used on the burr yew project (pages 126–7) are the ones to use for this one.

I have once again used a coved design around the rim to serve as a frame for the opening.

The redwood burr is an easy wood to work, and finishes well. The choice of gloss or matt finish is yours, but I prefer a matt finish for this wood.

The hollow form is dry-sanded down to 400 grit, finished with lemon oil and power-buffed to a fine finish.

tools used

¾in (19mm) spindle roughing gouge
⅜in (10mm) fingernail-profile spindle gouge
Straight hollowing tool with articulated tip
⅜in (10mm) beading and parting tool
⅛in (3mm) parting tool
Abrasive down to 400 grit
Lemon oil
Power-buffing mop loaded with EEE-Ultrashine

The underside shows an inset bead which is not included in the drawing. Decide which version you prefer

hints
● **The cheapest way of buying abrasives is in rolls. If you belong to a turning club, get together and buy some. The cost savings are large**
● **A 1in (25mm) sanding arbor is a handy thing to have to clean up the underside of work, especially if the bottom is recessed**

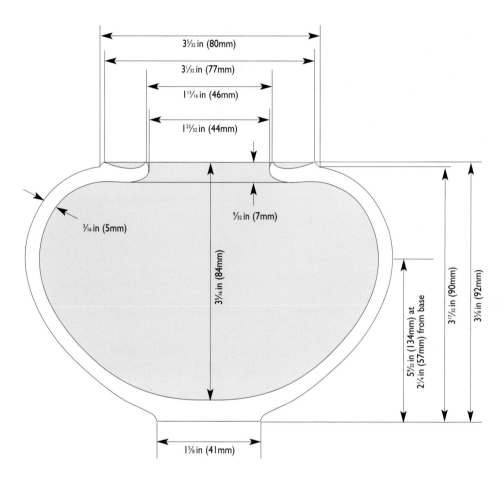

3⁵⁄₃₂ in (80mm)

3¹⁄₃₂ in (77mm)

1¹³⁄₁₆ in (46mm)

1²³⁄₃₂ in (44mm)

⁹⁄₃₂ in (7mm)

³⁄₁₆ in (5mm)

3⁵⁄₁₆ in (84mm)

5⁵⁄₃₂ in (134mm) at
2¼ in (57mm) from base

3¹⁷⁄₃₂ in (90mm)

3⅝ in (92mm)

1⅝ in (41mm)

grain
direction

alternative design

The shape is extended upwards to an almost egg-like body shape. There is also a raised foot that has a pointed internal section. As an alternative to the point, you could use a dome

10 pear form

American maple burr
Height: 3⅛in (79mm)
Diameter: 3¹⁷⁄₃₂in (90mm)

This is an example of a hollow form with a small opening. The grain is running spindle-wise, so the hollowing technique is the same as for the previous project. The big difference is that you will have to stop more often to clear out the shavings. Please check beforehand that the hollowing tool you have will fit through the opening; if not, scale up the project until it does. Pro rata, you will still be working through a small aperture.

This piece of wood has a very fine, tight grain and figuring, so it turned well without picking out.

The completed piece is dry-sanded down to 400 grit, finished with lemon oil and power-buffed using a mop loaded with carnauba wax for a higher shine. I experimented with satin and matt finishes, but the burr patterning was best shown off by a glossy finish.

tools used
¾in (19mm) spindle roughing gouge
⅜in (10mm) fingernail-profile spindle
    gouge
Straight hollowing tool with
    articulated tip
⅜in (10mm) beading and parting tool
⅛in (3mm) parting tool
Abrasive down to 400 grit
Lemon oil
Power-buffing mop loaded with
    carnauba wax

hints
● Make the hole through which you work at least 4mm (³⁄₁₆in) wider than the hollowing tool you are using
● Stop regularly to check the wall thickness

The base is small and slightly hollowed.
I made it just big enough to accommodate
my signature

scale: 100%

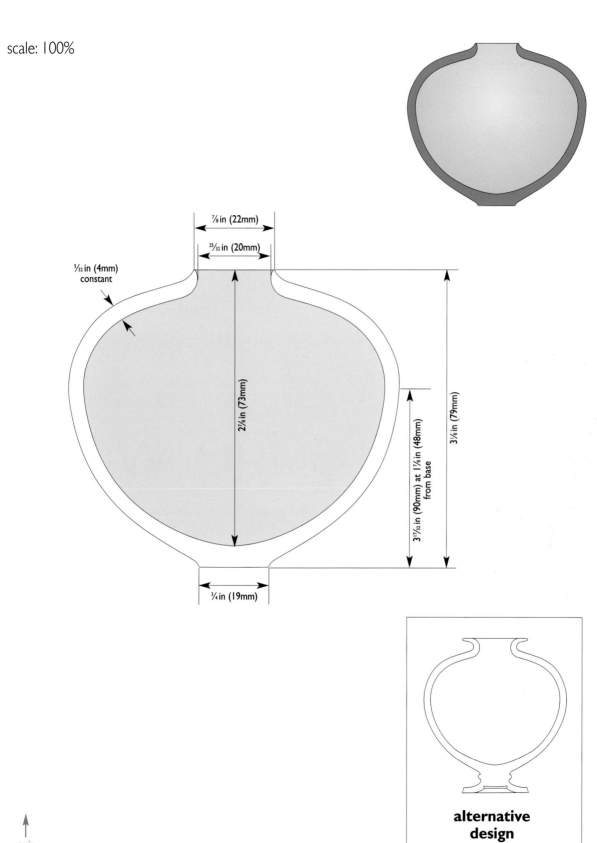

⁷⁄₈ in (22mm)

²⁵⁄₃₂ in (20mm)

⁵⁄₃₂ in (4mm)
constant

2⁷⁄₈ in (73mm)

3¹⁷⁄₂₁ in (90mm) at 1⁷⁄₈ in (48mm)
from base

3¹⁄₈ in (79mm)

¾ in (19mm)

grain
direction

**alternative
design**

A flared rim and a foot can
be added to good effect

natural-edge work

Natural-edge work is not restricted to bowls: boxes, hollow forms and other types of turning can also incorporate natural edges. I find this aspect of woodturning exciting, frustrating and challenging in equal measure.

The erratic nature of tree growth means that no two pieces are ever the same, so there are constant challenges, although the techniques for dealing with them are similar. Working to find a form that shows off the figure and grain in a piece of wood to their fullest is always fun, but on this type of work it is even more so. Will the bark inclusion form a void in the wall? If so, where will it be? Should you leave the bark on or off? All these questions and many more will occur as you turn. Some of the shapes you end up with may not work, but I guarantee you will enjoy working these things out.

6 nebula bowl

7 rectangular bowl

8 classical vase

9 gourd vase

10 pebble form

footed ogee bowl

apple
Height: approx. 2⅜in (60mm)
Diameter: approx. 4⅜in (110mm)

Natural-edge work is something that most turners will try, if only to see what can be made from an odd log that has sat in the corner of the workshop for ages. Natural-edge pieces do not have to be made from whole logs, where the grain is running parallel to the rotational axis of the lathe, as with spindles. They can also be made from wood that has the grain running at 90° to the axial rotation, as with most bowls.

This little project is an excellent introduction. Using a log of apple, we are going to make a small natural-edged bowl, and in this case the grain is running as in a spindle.

This is an unseasoned log, so we can explore the techniques of turning wet or green wood. Apple cuts well when dry, but, like most woods, it cuts exceptionally well when wet. Finishing, however, is less easy; we will look at techniques to overcome this.

Instead of using a roughing gouge followed by a spindle gouge, we will use a bowl gouge. The log is very out of true, and the toolrest may be a long way from where we need to work, so the extra blade thickness comes in very handy to reduce vibration. A spindle gouge will also be used, but only on the foot. The foot does not follow the convention of being between ⅓ and ½ of the overall diameter; instead, it is small and delicate, in keeping with the overall form.

The view from above emphasizes the irregularity of the log

hints
● The technique of shining light through the wood to reveal the wall thickness can be used on all forms of wet turning
● With natural-edge work I find it easier to apply the finish once the piece is off the lathe

tools used
½in (13mm) fingernail-profile bowl gouge with 45° bevel
⅜in (10mm) fingernail-profile spindle gouge
⅜in (10mm) beading and parting tool
³⁄₃₂in (2mm) fluted parting tool
Tipped shear scraper
Point tool
Carving tool (as available)
Abrasive down to 600 grit
Danish oil

scale: 100%

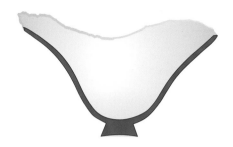

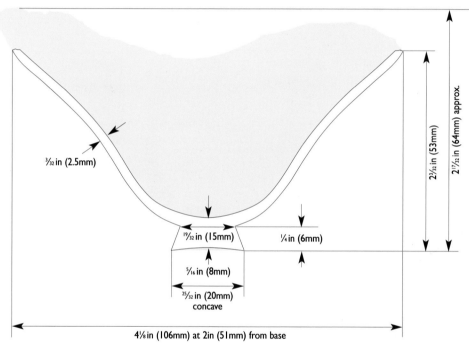

³⁄₃₂ in (2.5mm)

2³⁄₃₂ in (53mm)

2¹⁷⁄₃₂ in (64mm) approx.

¹⁹⁄₃₂ in (15mm)

¼ in (6mm)

⁵⁄₁₆ in (8mm)

²⁵⁄₃₂ in (20mm)
concave

4⅛ in (106mm) at 2in (51mm) from base

grain
direction

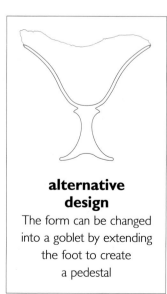

alternative design

The form can be changed into a goblet by extending the foot to create a pedestal

making the footed ogee bowl

1 Take a log of apple about 6in (150mm) diameter by 10in (250mm) long, find the centre of each end . . .

2 . . . and mount the log securely between centres. The drive centre is held in the jaws of the chuck, as shown in picture 1, and there is a revolving centre in the tailstock. Mounting the drive centre in the chuck saves you the trouble of removing the chuck when you need to use the centre

3 Now adjust the rest so that it is about ¼in (6mm) below centre and far enough away not to foul the wood when it is revolved by hand. Set the lathe to about 500rpm and, using a fingernail-profile bowl gouge, reduce a section of the log at the headstock end to a cylinder. Note how the *wing* of the gouge is presented to the work; the flute still points in the direction of travel, and the cut is made using the lower extended wing

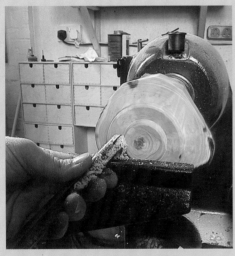

7 A few more cuts may be needed to remove any cracks and splits in the end of the log

8 Once you have produced a clean, flat face, move the rest again so that it is parallel to the outside of the log and far enough away not to foul it. Starting about ½in (13mm) down from the top edge of the blank, make a push cut towards the headstock . . .

9 . . . to remove the waste wood . . .

13 One final cut, and the form is determined

14 Bring the rest parallel with the flat top edge and increase the speed of the lathe to 1000rpm

15 Take the bowl gouge and start making arcing push cuts from the outer rim to the centre, creating the ogee form of the inside

4 Once a small area has been made cylindrical, take a beading and parting tool and cut a spigot to suit the jaws of your chuck

5 Now remove the log from between centres and mount it in the chuck, gripping it firmly by the spigot

6 Adjust the rest so it is parallel to the face of the work, and make a push cut with the gouge from the outer edge to the centre. The wet wood will produce long ribbons as you cut. Do not cut from centre to edge, or you risk dislodging the bark

10 ... and define the main body of the hollow form. Remember to cut *with* the grain, not against it

11 Continue this series of cuts, making your way back towards the chuck. Do not remove too much bulk from the chuck end, or you will get flexing at the other end

12 As you progress, adjust the rest to keep it as close to the work as possible without fouling

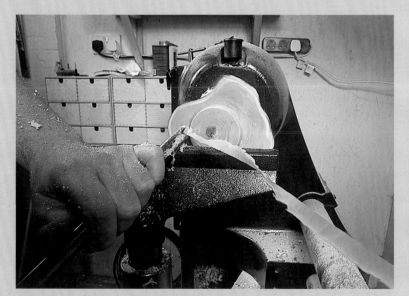

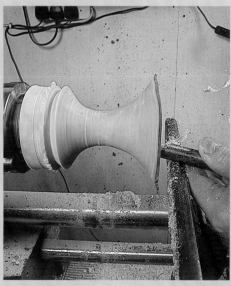

16 This is technically going against the grain, but if you were to cut from the centre to the rim you might well knock off the bark edge. By cutting this way, you minimize the risk of losing the bark. Because the wood is wet, it still cuts very cleanly

17 Very gentle refining cuts are needed as you near the required profile

If the piece were larger than this, you would not be able to make the finishing cuts from top to bottom. Instead, after removing most of the waste, work down in 1–2in (25–50mm) sections, finishing off each section before going on to the next. Working in this way, you will be able to achieve a uniform wall thickness without being hampered by flexing or distortion of the walls

18 Now shine a strong light – an adjustable lamp is ideal – on the side of the work. The light shining through the wet wood will allow you to judge the wall thickness. Thick areas show up as duller than the rest. When you have a uniform amount of light showing through the wall, then you have an even thickness

19 Now, using the curved edge of the tipped shear scraper, make a cut from the centre out toward the bark edge, but stopping *just before* the bark. The cutter is presented at about 45°

22 Once the main body is complete, you need to reduce the waste wood further down so you have room to create the foot

23 To ensure easy access, remove the wood down to quite a distance back from where the foot will be

24 Now take this part down to the diameter required for the foot

28 Sand the foot. Then, with the lathe slowed down to 300rpm, take a ¾₂in (2mm) fluted parting tool, which will make a cleaner cut than a conventional parting tool, and proceed to undercut the foot

29 A couple of cuts will be required to make the surface smooth

30 Once it has been undercut enough, hold the parting tool one-handed and hold the work with the other hand. Keeping hands and clothing away from the revolving wood and chuck, part off the bowl

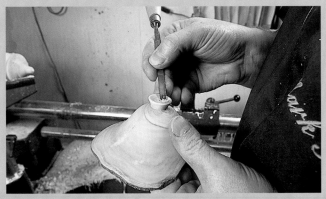

31 Use a carving tool to remove the pip . . .

32 . . . then power-sand the underside smooth. After a little wait to allow the wood to dry, rub it over with 600-grit abrasive to remove any raised grain, then apply Danish oil to the piece, and wipe the excess oil off after a few minutes with kitchen paper

20 Wet the wood with water and sand with wet and dry abrasive. Work through the grades down to 400 grit, using water as a lubricant throughout. Just wet the wood, don't soak it: water and electricity don't mix!

21 Now shine the lamp on the inside of the bowl, so the light shows through the ogee profile of the body. Take fine refining cuts with the bowl gouge until the wall thickness is uniform. Work from the rim down towards what will be the base, making light cuts so as not to dislodge the bark.

When cutting the bark edge, the gouge will not be in contact all the time. Do not apply too much pressure, and do not alter the initial angle of cut: you will soon be back into solid wood and have full bevel contact again

25 Wet-sand the outside form to the same standard as the inside

26 Now take a fingernail-profile spindle gouge and turn the foot

27 A point tool – a piece of HSS or carbon steel with three facets ground on the end like a wire nail – can be handy for getting into those hard-to-reach places such as the transition between body and foot.

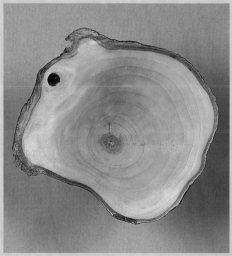

Two views of the finished bowl

2 crescent bowl

rowan
Height: approx. 2⁹⁄₁₆in (65mm)
Diameter: approx. 5⅞in (149mm)

This simple profile is created from a blank that has its grain running at 90° to the axial rotation of the lathe – in other words, crosswise like most bowls.

The centre of the blank is found, and it is then mounted between centres. The underside profile is cut (including a spigot at the tailstock end on which to hold it), sanded and oiled. The bowl is then reversed, mounted in a chuck, and the inside turned. When you try this project,

remember to use a push cut from the bark edge towards the inside or bottom of the work to avoid lifting off the bark.

Once the inside has been turned, sanded and oiled, the bowl is friction-driven between centres. A small, cloth-covered, dome-faced plywood disc attached on a screw chuck serves as the friction drive and supports the inside of the bowl. The spigot is then turned off (except the small central pip supported by the tailstock) and the bottom detailed. Once the piece is off the lathe, the pip is finally carved away and sanded to the same standard as the rest of the bowl.

A dense, close-grained wood with a fine bark, rowan is ideal for this kind of project. I have only ever found it available in small sections, so using the natural edge seems a nice way of avoiding waste.

This bowl is dry-sanded to 240 grit and finished with Hard Burnishing Oil.

The top view shows the creamy colour of rowan well. It also shows how, because there are two high points and two low points to the edge, the bowl looks oval. This optical illusion helps to disguise any distortion which may subsequently occur

hints

Cyanoacrylate is a handy product to have and use, but if used on one spot only it can stain, and may remain visible even after sanding and polishing.
To make it less conspicuous:
● When working on a bark edge, hold and tilt the bowl slightly so the bark side is pointing down. Apply the glue to the area concerned and then carry on all the way round so that the whole bark edge is treated
● When applying it to a crack, use a thin glue and sand the area immediately. The dust and the glue will mix together to create an effective filler that is less visible than glue alone
● To save money, store it in a fridge when not needed; this can extend the shelf life no end

tools used
⅜in (10mm) fingernail-profile bowl gouge
⅜in (10mm) beading and parting tool
Tipped shear scraper
⅛in (3mm) parting tool
³⁄₃₂in (2mm) fluted parting tool
Abrasive down to 240 grit
Hard Burnishing Oil

scale: 100%

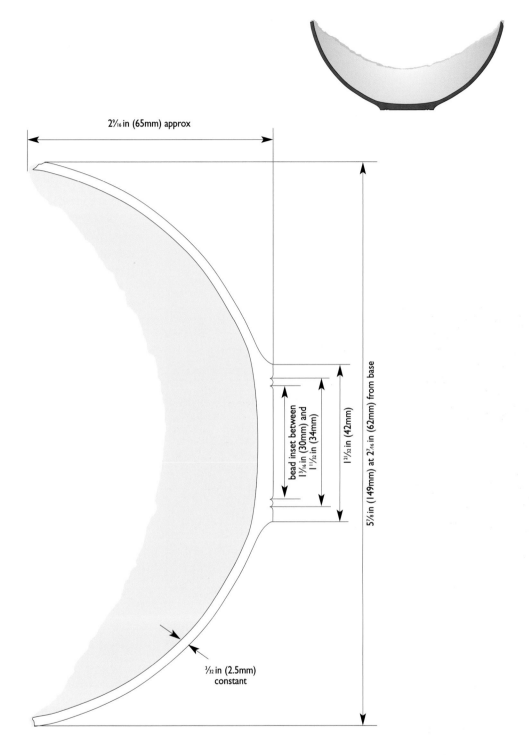

2⁹⁄₁₆ in (65mm) approx

bead inset between 1³⁄₁₆ in (30mm) and 1¹¹⁄₃₂ in (34mm)

1²¹⁄₃₂ in (42mm)

5⁷⁄₈ in (149mm) at 2⁷⁄₁₆ in (62mm) from base

³⁄₃₂ in (2.5mm) constant

direction
of grain

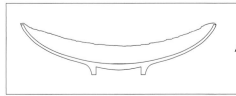

Alternative design
A shallower curve and a raised foot
can be used to good effect

3 jagged-edged bowl

European burr maple
Height: approx. 3⅝in (92mm)
Diameter: approx.10in (254mm)

Burrs of all sorts lend themselves to natural-edge work. The spiky exterior found on many burrs creates a dramatic edge. This piece also has the grain running crossways, so is turned in exactly the same way as the previous project.

This piece of maple burr was very nice to turn, but at 17% moisture content I knew it was not dry enough to avoid distortion. The interior is turned and completed in sections, as described in the panel on page 150, to minimize the effects of movement during the turning process. The finished piece is hand-oiled off the lathe. It has a 'hammered' or 'rippled' effect – I do not know if there is a technical term for this, but the burr figuring has shrunk, creating another pattern in the wood, clearly shown in the main photo, which I really like.

Finally, the bowl is dry-sanded to 400 grit and finished with lemon oil.

tools used
⅜in (10mm) fingernail-profile bowl gouge
⅜in (10mm) beading and parting tool
Tipped shear scraper
⅛in (3mm) parting tool
³⁄₂in (2mm) fluted parting tool
Abrasive down to 400 grit
Lemon oil

This view shows the full extent of the burr figuring. Again, high and low points of the edge create the illusion that the piece is not round

This view shows the detailing on the foot, and how the recessed foot can be used for signing your work

scale: 60%

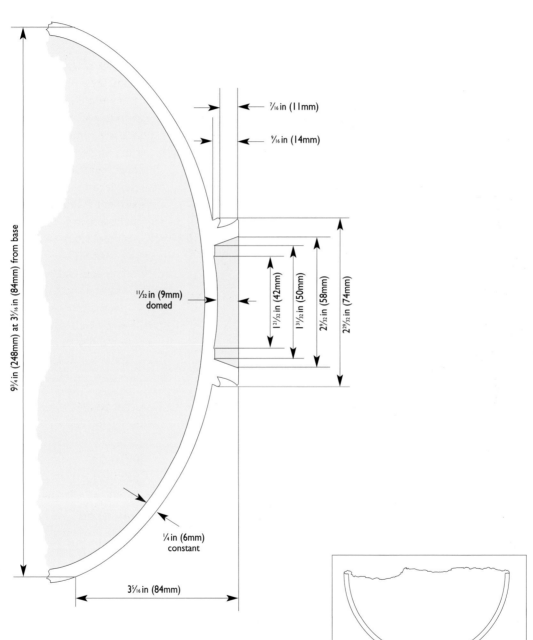

7/16 in (11mm)

9/16 in (14mm)

9¾ in (248mm) at 3⁵/₁₆ in (84mm) from base

11/32 in (9mm) domed

1 21/32 in (42mm)

1 31/32 in (50mm)

2 9/32 in (58mm)

2 29/32 in (74mm)

¼ in (6mm) constant

3⁵/₁₆ in (84mm)

grain direction

alternative design
The foot can be swept out and
made a little higher if you so wish

4 goblet vase

madrone burr
Height: 5–6in (127–152mm)
Diameter: 3⅜in (87mm)

This parallel-sided vase form has a foot that is about half the overall diameter. You will be working through a narrow opening, with the tools overhanging the rest quite a way, but it is not difficult to do. You will soon get used to how the tools feel when extended this far without support, and how to control them. This project also has the grain running the full length of the piece, spindle-wise. The procedure for mounting, working and finishing the project is the same as for the first piece in this section, except that you need to have a scraper or straight hollowing tool which is long enough to reach the bottom.

Madrone cuts well, and there is some beautiful striated figuring in this piece.

This bowl is dry-sanded to 400 grit, spray-finished with gloss acrylic lacquer and power-buffed to a fine finish. Again I have used a gloss finish, which shows off the burr figuring to the fullest extent.

A bead is added at the transition point between the main body and foot to create a visual break between the two sections

hints
● Have the power-buffing mop running in the opposite direction to the rotation of the lathe, and work in light, fluid movements
● Once you have loaded a mop with one compound, do not use it with anything else. If you want to use a mop for wax, for example, buy a new mop

tools used
¾in (19mm) spindle roughing gouge
⅜in (10mm) fingernail-profile spindle gouge
⅜in (10mm) beading and parting tool
Tipped shear scraper
⅛in (3mm) parting tool
³⁄₃₂in (2mm) fluted parting tool
Abrasive down to 400 grit
Spray gloss acrylic lacquer
Power-buffing mop loaded with EEE-Ultrashine

scale: 100%

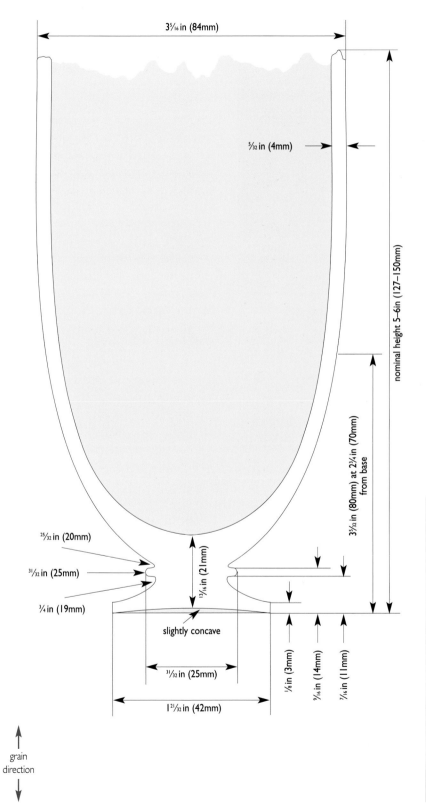

3⁵⁄₁₆ in (84mm)

⁵⁄₃₂ in (4mm)

nominal height 5–6in (127–150mm)

3⁵⁄₃₂ in (80mm) at 2¼ in (70mm) from base

²⁵⁄₃₂ in (20mm)

³¹⁄₃₂ in (25mm)

¾ in (19mm)

¹³⁄₁₆ in (21mm)

slightly concave

³¹⁄₃₂ in (25mm)

1²¹⁄₃₂ in (42mm)

⅛ in (3mm)

⁹⁄₁₆ in (14mm)

⁷⁄₁₆ in (11mm)

grain
direction

alternative design

Flare the rim out slightly to create a more open vase effect

5 fig-shaped box

red morell burr
Height: approx. 4¼in (108mm)
Diameter: 3in (76mm)

We all gather offcuts of wood in the workshop and say to ourselves that we will use them. This rarely happens, but here is a project that does use such offcuts. This box has a nice tactile body, contrasting with a spiky top which almost seems to offer protection for what is inside. The burr pattern is so dense that it is difficult to determine which way the grain runs, and in truth this is irrelevant: it cuts fine whichever way you work, but if you follow the principles of cutting used on spindles, you will be fine.

The methods described earlier for holding boxes apply to this piece also, but, because we have a natural-edged top to the lid, we cannot cut a spigot here to hold it. Instead, it is left as a cylinder and held in a chuck with extended jaws while the inside is turned. Once the inside of the lid is complete, this cylinder is mounted in the main box body while the neck detail is turned.

The box is dry-sanded to 400 grit and finished with lemon oil.

The underside is nice and smooth, and the base profile is curved. It is very stable when placed on a surface, and will not readily fall over if accidentally knocked

hints
● If you use wax on open-grained burrs you will end up with wax residue in the fissures. These take a lot of time to clean out, which is why I tend to use oils only on these types of burr
● Cordless power tools are great to use when power-sanding. There is no need to worry about leads getting caught in the work

tools used
¾in (19mm) spindle roughing gouge
⅜in (10mm) fingernail-profile spindle gouge
⅜in (10mm) beading and parting tool
⅛in (3mm) parting tool
³⁄₂in (2mm) fluted parting tool
Abrasive down to 400 grit
Lemon oil

scale: 100%

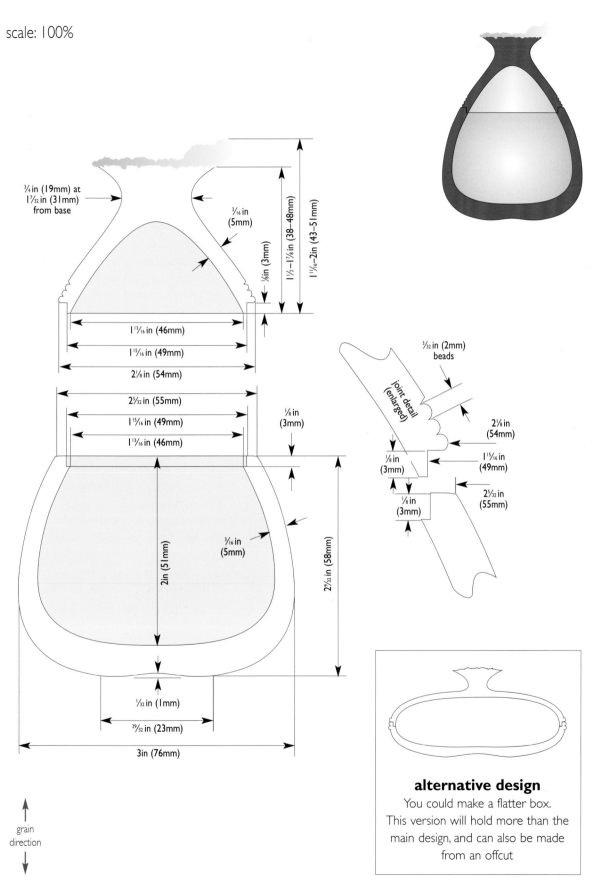

¾ in (19mm) at
1⁷⁄₃₂ in (31mm)
from base

³⁄₁₆ in
(5mm)

⅛ in (3mm)

1½–1⅞ in (38–48mm)

1¹¹⁄₁₆–2 in (43–51mm)

1¹³⁄₁₆ in (46mm)

1¹⁵⁄₁₆ in (49mm)

2⅛ in (54mm)

2⁵⁄₃₂ in (55mm)

1¹⁵⁄₁₆ in (49mm)

1¹³⁄₁₆ in (46mm)

⅛ in
(3mm)

³⁄₁₆ in
(5mm)

2 in (51mm)

2³⁄₃₂ in (58mm)

¹⁄₃₂ in (1mm)

²⁹⁄₃₂ in (23mm)

3 in (76mm)

grain
direction

³⁄₃₂ in (2mm)
beads

joint detail
(enlarged)

2⅛ in
(54mm)

⅛ in
(3mm)

1¹⁵⁄₁₆ in
(49mm)

⅛ in
(3mm)

2⁵⁄₃₂ in
(55mm)

alternative design

You could make a flatter box.
This version will hold more than the
main design, and can also be made
from an offcut

6 nebula bowl

goldfield burr
Height: 2⁹⁄₁₆in (65mm)
Width: approx. 10¾in (275mm)

This project is created and turned in the same way as the square bowl on pages 88–9. The fact that it has a natural edge makes very little difference to the processes required, but does mean that when it comes to creating the rim – which extends further on this piece – you will have to use very delicate cuts and freshly sharpened tools. On an irregular rim like this, there are times, out at the extremities, when the tool is in thin air more often than it makes contact with the wood. Have the rest parallel to the top face of the bowl, and keep traversing the tool parallel to the face at all times until you reach the upstanding coved and beaded fillet. This fillet frames the bowl and is undercut to create a shadow.

Australian burrs are usually sold as carbuncle-like sections in the UK, and are priced by weight. They can be quite expensive, but as a treat they are hard to beat for the beautiful figuring.

The bowl is dry-sanded to 400 grit, finished with lemon oil and power-buffed.

The very irregular edge provides a good contrast to the perfectly smooth bowl framed within it

This underside view shows the quirk that sets off the rim from the main body curve

tools used
⅜in (10mm) fingernail-profile bowl gouge
⅜in (10mm) beading and parting tool
⅛in (3mm) parting tool
³⁄₃₂in (2mm) fluted parting tool
Tipped shear scraper
1in (25mm) square-ended scraper
Abrasive down to 400 grit
Lemon oil
Power-buffing mop loaded with EEE-Ultrashine

scale: 60%

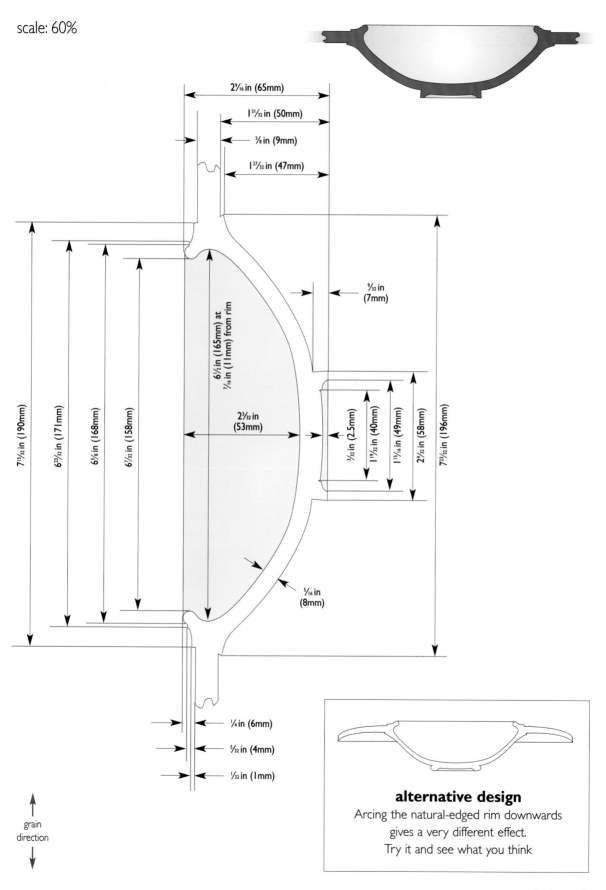

2⁹⁄₁₆ in (65mm)

1³¹⁄₃₂ in (50mm)

³⁄₈ in (9mm)

1²⁷⁄₃₂ in (47mm)

⁹⁄₃₂ in (7mm)

6½ in (165mm) at ⁷⁄₁₆ in (11mm) from rim

2³⁄₃₂ in (53mm)

³⁄₃₂ in (2.5mm)

1⁹⁄₃₂ in (40mm)

1¹⁵⁄₁₆ in (49mm)

2⁹⁄₃₂ in (58mm)

7²³⁄₃₂ in (196mm)

7¹⁵⁄₃₂ in (190mm)

6²³⁄₃₂ in (171mm)

6⅝ in (168mm)

6⁷⁄₃₂ in (158mm)

⁵⁄₁₆ in (8mm)

¼ in (6mm)

⁵⁄₃₂ in (4mm)

¹⁄₃₂ in (1mm)

grain
direction

alternative design
Arcing the natural-edged rim downwards
gives a very different effect.
Try it and see what you think

7 rectangular bowl

cherry
Height: 1⅞in (47mm)
Width: 8¾in (222mm)

Although turned from a log, this piece is mounted crosswise in the middle of the log between centres, so the grain runs from side to side. Mark the centre point on both sides, then mount the blank between centres. Turn the underside first, at 600rpm. The wing tips will be on the centre-line of the log, so do not cut beyond this when forming the bowl section. Make a spigot to allow reverse-mounting to turn the top. With the bowl part complete, use a pulling cut from the edge of the bowl towards the outer edge of the wing, making gentle arcing cuts to form the curvature. Use a domed scraper to clean up the wings. Do not sand yet.

With the spigot mounted in a chuck, turn the top face of the wings, using a push cut from the centre of the bowl out to the edge. The wings may flex if too much pressure is applied, so light cuts are needed. Once the thickness is uniform, smooth out any ripples with the square-ended scraper, then hollow out the bowl section. Sand the bowl, but not the wings.

The work is friction-driven between centres to remove the spigot and round the bottom, leaving a small pip in which the revolving centre is located. Sand the bottom of the bowl, but not the wings. Now remove it from the lathe, carve off the pip and sand smooth.

Power-sand the wings, being careful not to radius the edges. Hand-sand the underside where the bowl and wings meet, and then oil. If the ends of the wings are chipped, sand them on a belt sander. Dry-sand to 400 grit and apply lemon oil.

Cherry can have coloured streaks running through it, but this piece didn't. However, the pronounced grain patterns are very pretty

This is the bottom view. Look closely: had it not been pointed out, could you tell which was top and which was bottom?

hints
● When power sanding, keep the pad moving across the surface of the work. If you do not, you can sand hollows in the work and ruin the curve
● The bead can be formed in many ways: with a gouge or parting tool, or with a bead-forming tool, which can be bought from many manufacturers
● I am happy for the bowl to cant over slightly. If you want yours to stand straight, form a small flat on the base

tools used
⅜in (10mm) fingernail-profile bowl gouge
⅜in (10mm) beading and parting tool
⅛in (3mm) parting tool
³⁄₃₂in (2mm) fluted parting tool
Tipped shear scraper
1½in (38mm) shallow-domed end scraper
1½in (38mm) square-end scraper
Carving tool, as available
Abrasive down to 400 grit
Lemon oil

scale: 60%

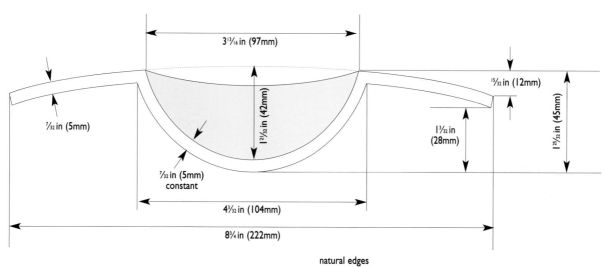

3¹³⁄₁₆ in (97mm)

¹⁵⁄₃₂ in (12mm)

⁷⁄₃₂ in (5mm)

1²¹⁄₃₂ in (42mm)

1²⁵⁄₃₂ in (45mm)

1³⁄₃₂ in (28mm)

⁷⁄₃₂ in (5mm) constant

4³⁄₃₂ in (104mm)

8¾ in (222mm)

natural edges

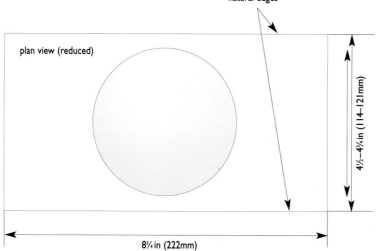

plan view (reduced)

4½–4¾ in (114–121mm)

8¾ in (222mm)

alternative design
An upward curve to the wings gives a more flower-like form and leads the eye into, rather than out of, the centre

grain direction

8 classical vase

horse chestnut burr
Height: approx. 5½in (142mm)
Diameter: 4⅜in (111mm)

This piece of horse chestnut burr was quite soft, so required sharp tools to get an even, clean cut.

The grain runs from side to side, but the piece is turned initially between centres, and the procedures already described for the egg-like hollow form on pages 126–7 are used here, except when it comes to friction-driving the piece to finish off the base. It is still friction-driven, but a cylinder of wood just smaller than the diameter of the opening and longer than the height of the vase is held in a chuck, and the vase is placed over this cylinder. A slight dome is formed on the end of the cylinder to match the curve on the inside of the vase. The tailstock with revolving centre is brought up for support, and then the piece can be worked in the normal way.

The quirk on the shoulder defines the body from the neck. It is large enough for the eye to see it, but not so large as to alter the curvature drastically.

The bowl is dry-sanded to 400 grit, finished with spray gloss acrylic lacquer and then power-buffed.

This view shows the opening, and how the bark inclusions have been incorporated in the design

hints
● **Do not be afraid of using coarse grades of abrasive if the wood requires it.** We should all aim to get the best finish we can from the tool, but it is not possible to get a great finish every time. Just start at the required grade and work through the grades to achieve the desired finish
● **You may find that you achieve a better cut with a scraper than with a gouge. If this is the case, use the scraper for profiling as well, if you have to**

tools used
⅜in (10mm) fingernail-profile bowl
    gouge
⅜in (10mm) beading and parting tool
Tipped straight hollowing tool
⅛in (3mm) parting tool
Abrasive down to 400 grit
Spray gloss acrylic lacquer
Power-buffing mop loaded with EEE-
    Ultrashine

scale: 75%

½₂ in (1mm)

shoulder
step detail
(enlarged)

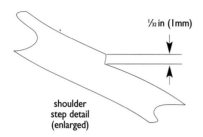

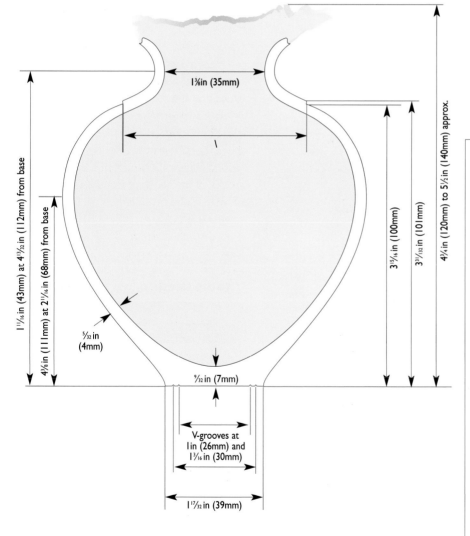

1⅜in (35mm)

1¹¹⁄₁₆ in (43mm) at 4¹³⁄₃₂ in (112mm) from base

4³⁄₈ in (111mm) at 2¹¹⁄₁₆ in (68mm) from base

⁵⁄₃₂ in
(4mm)

3¹⁵⁄₁₆ in (100mm)

3³¹⁄₃₂ in (101mm)

4¾ in (120mm) to 5½ in (140mm) approx.

⁹⁄₃₂ in (7mm)

V-grooves at
1 in (26mm) and
1³⁄₁₆ in (30mm)

1¹⁷⁄₃₂ in (39mm)

← grain →
direction

alternative design

A pedestal foot would raise the piece higher, and extending the neck would make for a more elegant shape. You could hollow this one through the neck, or you could join it as indicated at the transition point between neck and body. This would make turning the piece easier

9 gourd vase

burr oak
Height: approx. 6in (152mm)
Diameter: 7¹⁵⁄₃₂in (190mm)

Worked in the same way as the previous project, this piece is more bulbous and sits on a flat base, which gives a greater appearance of weightiness than a raised foot would do. The piece was wet-turned – about 23% moisture content to start with – then oiled and left to dry. There are undulations in the surface now where it has distorted and shrunk, but I like this effect and think it gives a piece added presence.

This piece of burr oak turned well: a good finish was obtained straight from the tool, and it required very little sanding. I like the variation in colour, and the way the texture changes from the tight pippy or knotty burr structure to the areas of swirling grain.

The completed vase is dry-sanded to 400 grit, finished with lemon oil and finally power-buffed.

The bottom has a small flat that is barely visible when viewed from underneath

hints
● **Oil may weep out of the fissures and holes in burr for some time after finishing. Never place a newly finished item directly on a piece of furniture unless there is a place mat underneath it**
● **If you need to stop part-way through a piece of wet turning, stuff the cavity full of the shavings you have just produced, place a plastic carrier bag over the piece and seal it with adhesive tap. This should prevent distortion for a little while**

tools used
⅜in (10mm) fingernail-profile bowl gouge
⅜in (10mm) beading and parting tool
Tipped straight hollowing tool
⅛in (3mm) parting tool
Abrasive down to 400 grit
Lemon oil
Power-buffing mop loaded with EEE-Ultrashine

scale: 60%

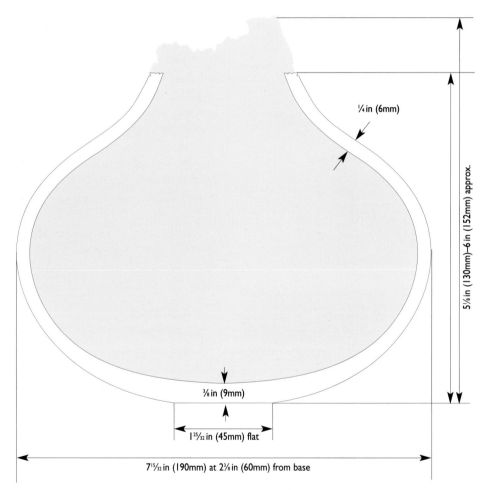

¼ in (6mm)

5⅛ in (130mm)–6 in (152mm) approx.

⅜ in (9mm)

1²⁵⁄₃₂ in (45mm) flat

7¹⁵⁄₃₂ in (190mm) at 2⅜ in (60mm) from base

grain
direction

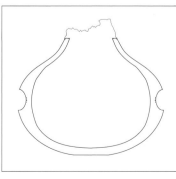

alternative design

If you wished, you could break up the
external curve by adding a detail at the
widest part, such as this cove with small
beads inside. The wall thickness needs to be
slightly thicker at this part, but then the great
majority of it will be removed as the
detail is formed

10 pebble form

false acacia burr
Height: 4¼in (108mm)
Diameter: 10⅝in (262mm)

This piece of false acacia burr has some of the most beautiful markings I have ever seen. The tight, pippy burr is a delight to turn, as well as to look at. Yet more visual interest is provided by the contrast between the yellow heartwood and the cream sapwood, and by the bark inclusions creating voids in the sidewalls.

Use the same turning sequence as described for the she-oak hollow form on pages 120–5, except for the reverse-chucking, where you will have to use a cylinder for support, as described on page 164. This is passed through the opening at the top and rested on the bottom of the cavity to provide the friction drive when the piece is reversed in order to turn away the foot.

This hollow form is dry-sanded to 400 grit and then finished with lemon oil.

The bark inclusions which give rise to voids in the walls are shown clearly from this angle

tools used
⅜in (10mm) fingernail-profile bowl
        gouge
⅜in (10mm) beading and parting tool
Tipped straight hollowing tool
Swan-neck hollowing tool
⅛in (3mm) parting tool
³⁄₃₂in (2mm) fluted parting tool
Abrasive down to 400 grit
Lemon oil

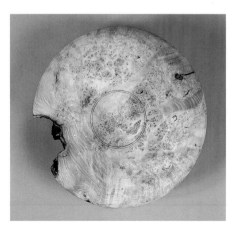

The underside has a dome and a small bead where the spigot was

scale: 60%

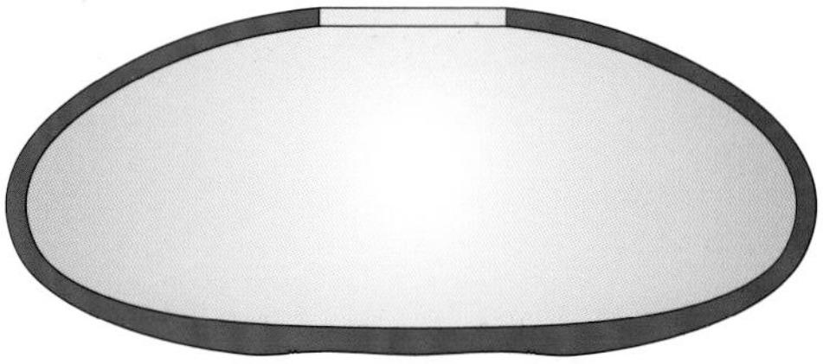

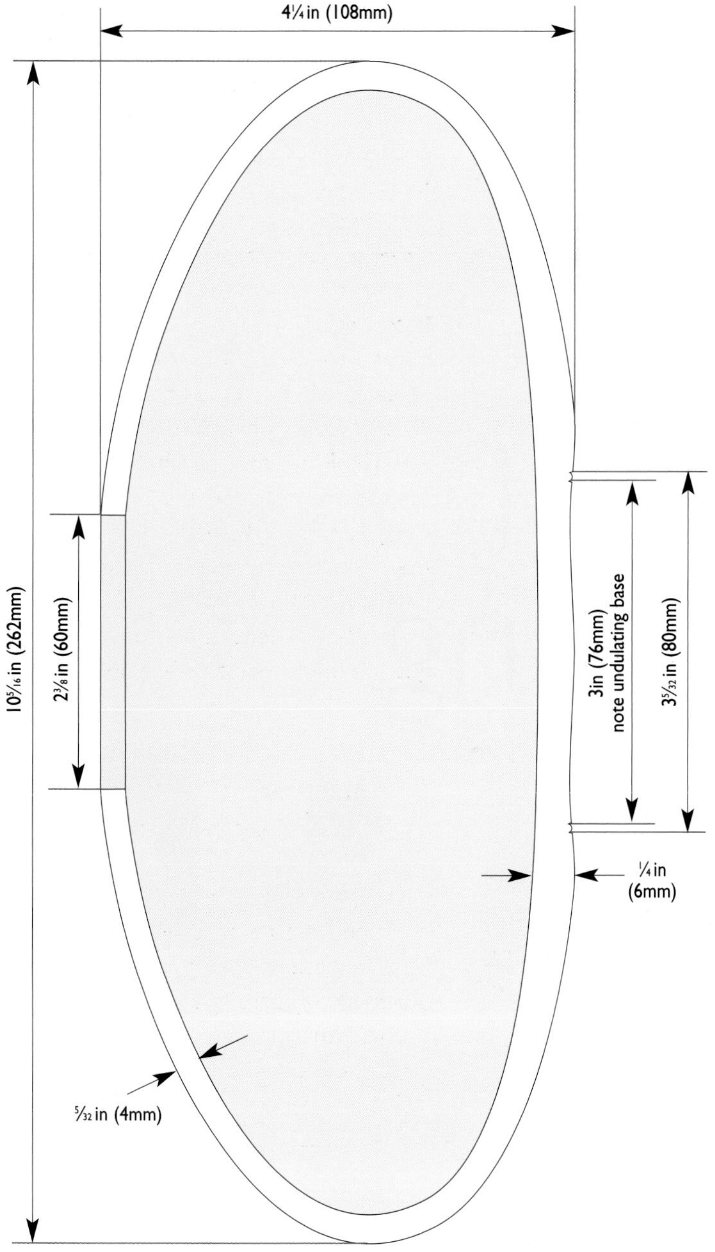

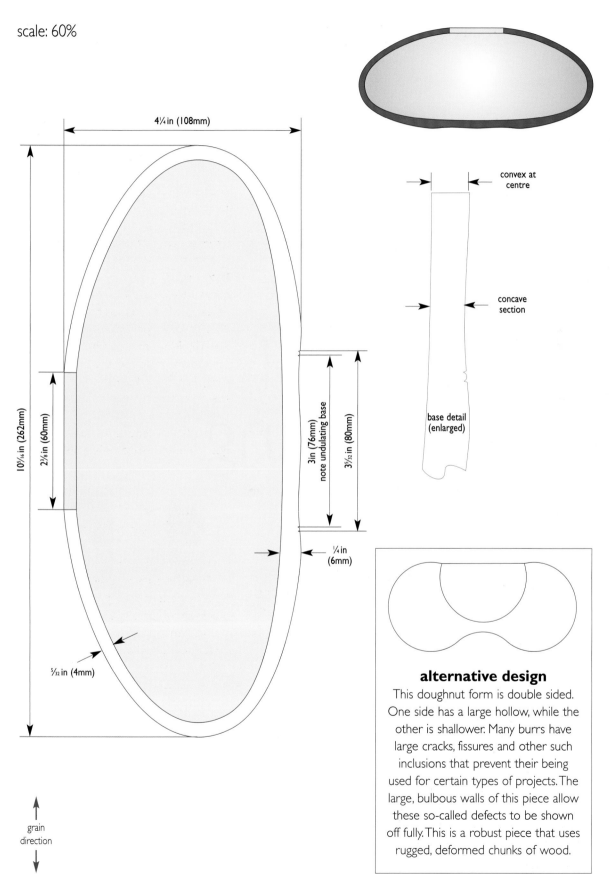

$4\frac{1}{4}$ in (108mm)
$10\frac{5}{16}$ in (262mm)
$2\frac{3}{8}$ in (60mm)
3in (76mm)
note undulating base
$3\frac{5}{32}$ in (80mm)
$\frac{1}{4}$ in
(6mm)
$\frac{5}{32}$ in (4mm)

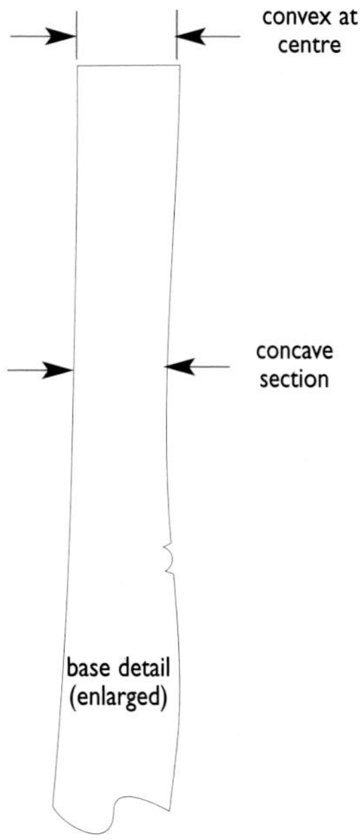

convex at
centre
concave
section
base detail
(enlarged)

grain
direction

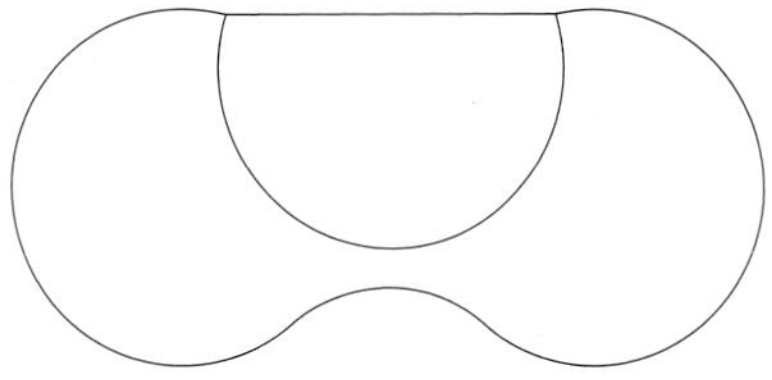

alternative design

This doughnut form is double sided. One side has a large hollow, while the other is shallower. Many burrs have large cracks, fissures and other such inclusions that prevent their being used for certain types of projects. The large, bulbous walls of this piece allow these so-called defects to be shown off fully. This is a robust piece that uses rugged, deformed chunks of wood.

a gallery of woodturning

It is always a pleasure to look at other turners' work and share ideas and thoughts with them. I always pick up valuable suggestions and new techniques, and I appreciate the willingness to share that is usual among turners worldwide. Taking time to study the work of masters of their craft will bring rich rewards. The following pages offer a selection of inspiring work from some internationally known turners.

ray key

page 172

bert marsh

page 174

stuart
mortimer

gary rance

chris stott

john hunnex

allan
beecham

Enclosed vessels

Spalted beech

Height: 7in (180mm)

Diameter: 5½in (140mm)

(tallest piece)

ray key

Ray is an internationally respected turner, teacher, demonstrator and author, whose work I have admired for many years. He has a fantastic eye for making strong, striking forms from pure, uncomplicated shapes. They look simple to make, but are anything but. These beautifully understated forms show off the work, the wood and the skill of the turner to the fullest.

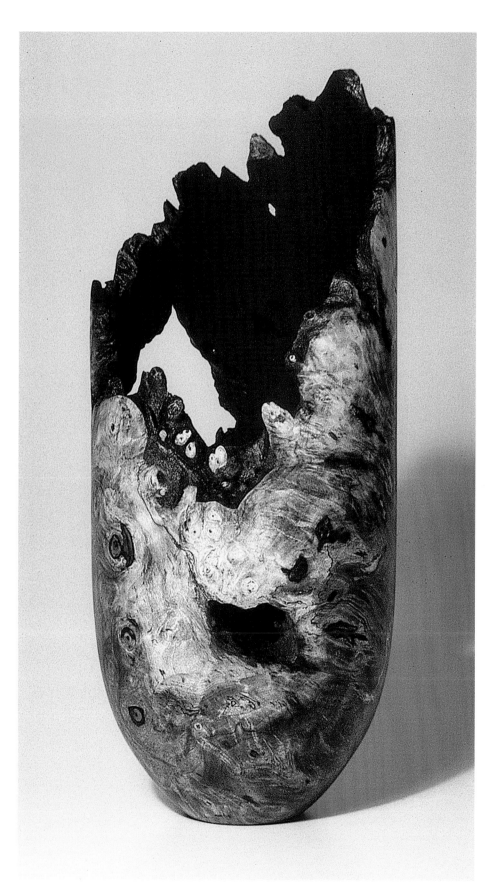

U-shaped vessel
Buckeye burr
Height: 10¾in (270mm)
Diameter: 5⅛in (130mm)

Natural-edge bowl

Burr elm

bert marsh

Known internationally as a turner, teacher, demonstrator and author, Bert is one of the most highly qualified woodworkers I know. He has always been willing to share his time and knowledge with others. His mastery of turning is sheer joy to behold, and Bert's delicate, graceful forms command attention.

Natural-edge bowl

Laburnum

Leaf-shaped platter

Scottish burr elm

Length: 28in (710mm)

Width: 20in (510mm)

stuart mortimer

Stuart's career encompasses writing about woodturning as well as teaching and demonstrating on both sides of the Atlantic, but he is probably best known today for his wonderful work involving twists and carved lace rims on hollow forms. However, adornment of such kind is not always his modus operandi. Stuart, like all turners, loves to explore form and see which shapes work, and why.

Natural-edged bowl

Scottish burr elm

Diameter: 22in (560mm)

Height: 9in (230mm)

This was the largest in

a nest of five bowls

Natural-edge platter

Lime burr

Diameter: 14in (355mm)

gary rance

Gary is a time-served turner who is just as happy turning a batch of functional newel posts as he is creating aesthetic gallery pieces. He demonstrates internationally, and has an eye for detail that is awe-inspiring. Not only that, but he is one of the fastest turners I know.

Pair of lidded chalices

Oak

Height: 10in (254mm)

Four-stack box

Ripple ash

Height: 4¹⁷⁄₃₂in (115mm)

Diameter: 2⁹⁄₁₆in (65mm)

chris stott

I would not say that Chris specializes in any one type of turning; instead, he is able to turn his hand to most aspects and create work that is wonderful to touch, always well proportioned and impeccably well finished. He demonstrates and teaches internationally, and is well known as a writer on turning and author of instructional videos on the subject.

Elegant box

Olive

Height: 2$^{25}/_{32}$in (71mm)

Diameter: 3$^{13}/_{16}$in (97mm)

**Natural-edge
hollow form**
Maple burr
Height: 6in (152mm)
Diameter: 13in (330mm)

john
hunnex

J ohn is a turner and author who loves
to experiment with shapes, especially
hollow forms. Never satisfied with what
he has created, he is always working out
ways to do things quicker and better, and
exploring how contrasting shapes work
together to create something special.

Hollow form

Brown oak burr

Height: 8in (203mm)

Diameter: 10in (254mm)

Semi-enclosed bowl

Figured claro walnut

allan beecham

Allan is a traditionally trained turner who is happy to tackle most turning jobs, and probably has. He works fast and accurately, and has a truly wonderful clarity of thought and technique.

Hollow form

Elm

useful contacts

I have given contact details for suppliers and manufacturers whose products I have used in the book. There are many others which I do not have space to mention; you will find them in local directories and woodworking magazines.

Ashley Iles (Edge Tools) Ltd., East Kirkby, Spilsby, Lincolnshire, PE23 4DD, England
Tel: 01790 763372
Fax: 01790 763610
Email: sales@ashleyiles.co.uk
Website: www.ashleyiles.co.uk
Turning tools

Australian Outback Imports, Unit 4, Rolts Garden Centre, Clacton Road, Elmstead Market, Colchester, Essex, CO7 7DD, England
Tel: 01206 826602
Website:
www.ozoutbackimports.com
Wood, turning accessories, sanding ball

Axminster Power Tool Centre, Chard Street, Axminster, Devon, EX13 5DZ, England
Tel: 01297 33656/0800 371822
Fax: 01297 35242
Email: email@axminster.co.uk
Website: www.axminster.co.uk
Lathes, turning tools, wood

BriMarc Associates, 8 Ladbroke Park, Millers Road, Warwick, CV34 5AE, England
Tel: 01926 493389
Email: sales@brimarc.com
Turning tools, lathes, accessories

BWS (Barmossie Woodturning), Moss of Barmuckity, By Elgin, IV30 8QW, Scotland
Tel: 01343 842678
Wood

C. & M. O'Donnell, Brough, Thurso, Caithness, KW14 8YE, Scotland
Tel: 01847 851605
Fax: 01847 851793
Email: info@woodturning.uk.com
Website: www.woodturning.uk.com
Turning accessories

Chestnut Products, PO Box 536, Ipswich, IP4 5WN, England
Tel: 01473 425878
Fax: 01473 431096
Email: mailroom@chestnutproducts.co.uk
Website: www.chestnutproducts.co.uk
Finishing products

Craft Supplies Ltd, The Mill, Millers Dale, Nr Buxton, Derbyshire, SK17 8SN, England
Tel: 01298 871636
Fax: 01298 872263
Email: sales@craft-supplies.co.uk
Website: www.craft-supplies.co.uk
Lathes, turning accessories, wood

Craft Supplies USA, 1287 E 1120 S, Provo, UT 84608, USA
Phone: (800) 551 8876
FAX: 801 377 7742
E-Mail: service@woodturnerscatalog.com
Website: www.woodturnerscatalog.com
Lathes, turning tools, accessories

Crown Hand Tools Ltd, Excelsior, Burnt Tree Lane, Hoyle St, Sheffield, S3 7EX, England
Tel: 0114 272 3366
Fax: 0114 272 5252
Email: info@crownhandtools.com
Website: www.crownhandtools.com
Turning tools

Glaser Engineering Co., PO Box 95, El Segundo, CA 90245, USA
001 310 823 7128
Fax 310 823 7889
Email: jglaserwt@aol.com
Turning tools, accessories

Grip-a-Disc, Jill Piers Woodturning Supplies, 2 Kimberly Villas, Southmill Road, Bishops Stortford, Herts, CM23 3DW, England
Tel/Fax: 01279 653760
Abrasives

Hamlet Craft Tools, Units 21–24, Penistone Road Industrial Estate, Sheffield, S6 2FL, England
Tel: 0114 232 1338
Fax: 0114 232 5794
Email: sales@hamlet-crafttools.com
Website: www.hamlet-crafttools.com
Turning tools

Henry Taylor (Tools) Ltd., Peacock Estate, Livesey Street, Sheffield, S6 2BL, England
Tel: 0114 234 0282/0321
Fax: 0114 285 2015
Email: sales@henrytaylortools.co.uk
Website: www.henrytaylortools.co.uk
Turning tools

John Bradford, Burcombe Flower Farm, Wiggaton, Ottery St Mary, Devon, EX11 1PU, England
Tel: 01404 814533
Wood

Kelton Industries Ltd, PO Box 589, Kaitaia 500, New Zealand
Tel/Fax: 9 408 5862
Email: info@kelton.co.nz
Website: www.kelton.co.nz
Turning tools, accessories

Liberon Waxes Ltd, Mountfield Industrial Estate, Learoyd Road, New Romney, Kent, TN28 8XU, England
Tel: 01797 367555
Fax: 01797 367575
Finishing products

Multistar Woodturning Systems, 4
Holledge Crescent, Frinton-on-Sea,
Essex. CO13 0RW, England
Tel: 01255 676026
Website: www.multistardirect.com
Turning accessories

Oneway Manufacturing, 241
Monteith Ave., Stratford, Ontario,
N5A 2P6, Canada
Phone: 1 519 271 7611
Toll-free (USA and Canada only):
1 800 565 7288
Fax: 1 519 271 8892
Website: www.oneway.ca
Lathes, turning tools, accessories

Organoil Pty Ltd, Lot 4, Centennial
Circuit, PO Box 377, Byron Bay,
NSW, Australia
Tel: 02 6685 8896
Fax: 02 6685 6747
Email: mail@organoil.com.au
Website: www.organoil.com.au
Finishing products

Performance Abrasives, 7533 Easy
Street, Mason, OH 45040, USA
Tel: 513 754 1022
Fax: 513 754 1025
Abrasives

Peter Child, The Old Hyde, Little
Yeldham, Nr Halstead, Essex, CO9
4QT, England
Tel: 01787 237291
Fax: 01787 238522
Website: www.peterchild.co.uk
Turning tools, lathes, wood

Record Power Ltd., Parkway Works,
Sheffield, S9 3BL, England
Tel: 0114 251 9102
Fax: 0114 261 7141
Email:
recordpower@recordtools.co.uk
Website: www.recordpower.co.uk
Lathes, turning tools, accessories

Robert Sorby, Athol Road, Sheffield,
S8 0PA, England
Tel: 0114 225 0700
Fax: 0114 225 0710
Email: sales@robert-sorby.co.uk
Website: www.robert-sorby.co.uk
Lathes, turning tools, accessories

Stiles & Bates, Upper Farm, Church
Hill, Sutton, Dover, Kent, CT15 5DF,
England
Tel/Fax: 01304 366360
Email: courses@stilesandbates.co.uk
Website: www.stilesandbates.co.uk
Wood

T&J Tools, 14 Main Street,
Willoughby, Warwickshire, CV23
8BH, England
Tel: 01788 890121
Email: info@t-jtools.co.uk
Website: www.j-tools.co.uk
Turning accessories

U-Beaut Products
Tel: (Australia) 03 5221 8775
Email: ubeaut@ubeaut.com.au
Website: www.ubeaut.com.au
Finishing products

VB Manufacturing, Unit 8, North
Crescent, Diplocks Way, Hailsham,
East Sussex, BN27 3JF, England
Tel: 0800 064 4180
Website: www.hegner.co.uk
Lathes, accessories

Vicmarc Machinery, 52 Grice Street,
Clontarf, Qld 4350, Australia
Tel: 7 3284 3103
Fax: 7 3283 4656
Email: vicmarc@vicmarc.com
Website: http://www.vicmarc.com
Lathes, accessories

VM-UK Ltd, Unit F, Rough Farm
Industrial Estate, Atherstone on
Stour, Stratford on Avon,
Warwickshire, CV37 8DX, England
Tel/Fax: 01789 459262
Email: pjirons@globalnet.co.uk
Turning tools, lathes, accessories

Woodchucker's Supplies, 1698
Weston Road, Weston, Ontario,
M9N 1V6, Canada
Tel: 1 800 551 0192/416 241 8654
Fax: 416 241 8656
Email: sales@woodchuckers.com
Website: www.woodchuckers.com
*Turning tools, lathes, accessories, Astra
Dot abrasive*

Woodcraft Supply Corp, PO Box
1686, Parkersburg, WV 26102-1686,
USA
Tel: (304) 422 5412
Website: www.woodcraft.com
Turning tools, lathes, accessories

Yandle & Sons Ltd, Hurst Works,
Martock, Somerset, TA12 6JU,
England
Tel: 01935 822207
Fax: 01935 824484
Wood

further reading

books

Chapman, Robert, *Woodturning: A Fresh Approach* (Lewes, East Sussex: GMC Publications, 1999)
ISBN 1 86108 119 7

Hoadley, R. Bruce, *Understanding Wood: A Craftsman's Guide to Wood Technology* (Newtown, CT: Taunton Press, 2000)
ISBN 1 56158 358 8

Hunnex, John, *Woodturning: A Source Book of Shapes* (Lewes, East Sussex: GMC Publications, 1993)
ISBN 0 946819 45 9

—, *Woodturning: Forms and Materials* (Lewes, East Sussex: GMC Publications, 2003)
ISBN 1 86108 355 6

Jackson, Lesley, *20th-Century Factory Glass* (London: Mitchell Beazley, 2000)
ISBN 1 85732 267 3

Key, Ray, *Woodturning with Ray Key* (London: Batsford, 1998)
ISBN 0 7134 8149 8

O'Donnell, Michael, *Turning Green Wood* (Lewes, East Sussex: GMC Publications, 2000)
ISBN 1 86108 089 1

Raffan, Richard, *Turned-Bowl Design* (Newtown, CT: Taunton Press, 1998)
ISBN 0 918804 82 5

—, *Turning Boxes with Richard Raffan*, revised edition (Newtown, CT: Taunton Press, 2002)
ISBN 1 56158 509 2

Rowley, Keith, *Woodturning: A Foundation Course*, new edition (Lewes, East Sussex: GMC Publications, 1999)
ISBN 1 86108 114 6

Stott, Chris, *Turned Boxes: 50 Designs* (Lewes, East Sussex: GMC Publications, 2002)
ISBN 1 86108 203 7

videos

Ellsworth, David, *Tips for Turners: Hollow Turning* (Lewes, East Sussex: GMC Publications)
ISBN 1 86108 260 6

Jordan, John, *Hollow Turning* (Lewes, East Sussex: GMC Publications)
ISBN 0 946819 81 5

Key, Ray, *Turned Boxes* (Lewes, East Sussex: GMC Publications); a series of three videos: *The Basic Box* ISBN 1 86108 024 7; *The Capsule Box* ISBN 1 86108 025 5; *The Finial Box* ISBN 1 86108 026 3

Stott, Chris, *A Lesson with Chris Stott: Natural Edges & Hollow Forms* (Lewes, East Sussex: GMC Publications)
ISBN 1 86108 029 8

Stubbs, Del, *Bowl Turning with Del Stubbs* (Newtown, CT: Taunton Press)
ISBN 0 918804 36 1

about the author

Mark Baker has always been fascinated by wood. The ability to work with such a wonderful medium, and to create something that will be admired, is fantastic, despite the occasional frustrations.

His father and a couple of uncles were carpenters and joiners, and, on leaving school, Mark in turn served a five-year apprenticeship in carpentry and joinery with a local building firm, where the duties included restoration work. He then helped to set up an industrial workshop for autistic adults. He obtained qualifications in teaching adults with special needs, and attained the level of Senior Instructor. Following this, he went to work as product manager for one of the major manufacturers of woodturning tools in Sheffield. From here, he was headhunted to be the editor of GMC's *Woodturning* magazine, and in addition he is now Group Editor of GMC's whole range of craft magazines.

He has demonstrated in the USA, Canada and Europe, and loves meeting turners from around the world.

index